LETTERS FROM AMHERST

ALSO BY SAMUEL R. DELANY

SAMUEL R. DELANY

. . .

Letters from Amherst

FIVE NARRATIVE LETTERS

Iva Hacker-Delany

WESLEYAN UNIVERSITY PRESS

Middletown, Connecticut

Wesleyan University Press
Middletown CT 06459
www.wesleyan.edu/wespress
© 2019 Samuel R. Delany
All rights reserved
Manufactured in the United States of America
Designed by Richard Hendel
Typeset in Utopia and Hertz by Passumpsic Publishing

Library of Congress Cataloging-in-Publication Data available upon request

Hardcover ISBN: 978-0-8195-7820-4
Paperback ISBN: 978-0-8195-7851-8
Ebook ISBN: 978-0-8195-7821-1

5 4 3 2 1

FRONTISPIECE

Iva Hacker-Delany (bottom left): Graduation picture from the Bronx High School of Science. Chip Delany (center): Taken in the first week of teaching at UMass in 1988. Chip Delany (top right) at Noreascon 3 in Boston, August 31, 1989.

Never was a work—if it can be called a work—less planned and less contrived than these . . . letters written at longish intervals, almost always in the throes of some emotional crisis which they reflect without actually describing. They were for me no more than a natural and instinctive relief from worries, hardships or despondencies that made it impossible for me to start or continue writing a novel. Some were even written at great speed, broken off abruptly to catch the mail and posted without any thought of publication. Later the idea of putting them together and filling up the gaps made me reclaim them from those friends most likely to have preserved my epistles; and these are the ones which are possibly the least unworthy—understandably enough, since we are always more open and at ease when talking about our feelings to one person in private than in the presence of someone unknown. That unknown third party is the reader, the public; and were it not that writing has a definite appeal—often painful, sometimes intoxicating, but ever irresistible—which makes us forget the unknown witness and be carried away by our topic, I don't think we would ever have the courage to write about ourselves—unless we had a great deal of good to say. . . . And may the lovers of fiction not judge me too severely either.

GEORGE SAND, *Lettres d'un voyageur*

CONTENTS

CORRESPONDENTS

ROBERT S. BRAVARD

was director of library services at the Stevenson Library at
Lock Haven University, Lock Haven, Pennsylvania, and the coauthor
with Michael W. Peplow of *Samuel R. Delany, A Primary and
Secondary Bibliography, 1962–1979* (G. K. Hall, 1980).

KATHLEEN SPENCER

is the author of a monograph, *Charles Williams*
(Starmont, 1985), and was a professor of English at the
University of Nebraska, Lincoln.

ERIN MCGRAW

is author of the short story collections *Bodies at Sea*
(University of Illinois Press, 1989) and *Lies of the Saints*
(Chronicle Books, 1996), and the novel *The Baby Tree*
(Story Line Press, 2002). She taught English at DePauw University
and Ohio State University.

FOREWORD

Nalo Hopkinson

In 2014, the Damon Knight Memorial Grand Master Award was presented to Samuel R. Delany. In science fiction and fantasy literary circles, this award confers recognition and respect to someone whose oeuvre is of significant merit. It may have been the first time in the award's thirty-eight years of existence that it went to a writer of color; certainly it was the first time it was conferred upon a Black writer. Delany has written in numerous genres, but we in science fiction claim him and he claims us — certainly not a monogamous relationship, but a strong and loyal one — so I write about him from that perspective.

I've been reading Samuel "Chip" Delany's work since I was in my 20s, long before I came to know him personally. I began with his science fiction and fantasy, since that's my preferred mode of fiction (and which, a decade or so later I would choose as the mode in which I primarily write. It was in Chip's work that I encountered the concept that science fiction is not a genre with a single, fixed narrative, but a "metagenre." It's more a way of writing and reading; what I now call a "mode" of writing.).

When I'd read all of Chip's science fiction and fantasy I could get my hands on, I was still craving more of his words, so when I discovered his non-fiction, I moved on to that. His autobiographies *Heavenly Breakfast* and *The Motion of Light in Water* were a jaw-dropping revelation. They were evidence of a person living a life outside the mainstream, and not simply living it, but also finding friends, allies, lovers, love and support along the way. Those two books showed me that I too, a misfit Black girl, could dare to live.

Those read, I moved on to Chip's scholarly work. Not a familiar leap for me at all; at the time, more than thirty years ago, I read fiction almost exclusively.

I didn't know what to expect, had no idea what I'd let myself in for. Chip provided one of my first introductions to the scholarly practices of cultural theory and literary criticism. Many of the concepts were completely new to me. I barely grasped half of what I read. But the ideas, the lovely, shiny ideas and Chip's plum-cake-rich writing style, luxuriating as it does in words, connections, *detail*, and precision, captured me in prisms, mirrors, lenses, and kept (keeps) me reading. Yes, it's a mixed metaphor. It's all right; you'll survive.

What's more, for all Chip's evident erudition when he's writing this way, he can be playful about it. In this volume you'll find a letter in which he talks about having just finished "a new Steiner essay." He's referring to his alternate ego, a woman scholar he's invented and named Leslie K. Steiner. She writes criticism of Samuel R. Delany's writing.

The man deconstructs and critiques his own fiction, and does so unflinchingly. When I first discovered that, I was both awed and amused —still am.

The first time I met Chip in person was quite a brief encounter. He was in my then home town of Toronto, Canada, being interviewed by Judy Merril. Judy is the person who introduced me to the practice of the informal writing workshop by encouraging me and a number of other would-be students of hers to form one. Chip talks about her in the first letter in this book. She was a writer, editor, and all-round inciter, a powerful and positive influence in science fiction and fantasy. I'm now friends and have occasional writing dates with Judy's granddaughter, the talented Emily Pohl-Weary. It is thus that these connections extend through the generations.

In any case, I attended the interview. Afterwards, Chip did a signing. I shyly handed him my copy of his novel *Dhalgren*. It was a library discard, already battered before it came into my hands. My own multiple readings of the book had rendered it threadbare as a well-loved teddy bear by the time I presented it to him. Its ears had been dogged and nibbled upon. There were old library stickers on it. There may even have been water damage to some of its pages. I apologized for the state of the book and for not having bought my own new copy of it (I did understand how royalties work, and I knew that artists need to get paid. But the book wasn't in print at the time, and nevertheless, my book budget was quite limited.) I believe Chip generously replied that what was important was that I'd read it. I agree. Nowadays, it's what I say to readers who apologize to me for having obtained my books through their local public libraries. Many years later, when I was first getting to know the person who would become my primary life partner, he talked about having had a very similar encounter with Chip. The fact that my swain was a fellow Black person who also knew and adored Delany's writing was a huge checkmark in the "positive" column of my mental pros and cons list for pursuing the relationship. I suspect he felt the same way. (And now my mischievous brain is whispering, "Chip Delany as hanky code! Write that down!" So I am.)

As I watched Chip interact with his readers at that signing, I realized —a bit to my surprise, I admit—that the way he deals with people in person is, well, personable. I guess I'd expected him to speak the way he writes; in long, complex, deeply erudite sentences. He doesn't. He speaks plainly and respectfully, and accords worthiness to everyone at first blush. I would later learn that he doesn't suffer fools, but his bluntest of ripostes are delivered as though to an equal.

The same personableness is evident in the five letters which comprise this book. The strongest impression I came away with from reading it; Chip likes people. He cares deeply for his friends, lovers, family, students, and strangers. He loves watching his friends fall in love. He loves cooking for them. He loves talking with his daughter, and has done since she was a child. He has long conversations with strangers he meets on public transit. That's a difficult thing for me to do.

I very much enjoyed reading his stories about meeting and falling in love with his partner Dennis. I knew bits of them already, from having read the autobiographical comic he did with artist Mia Wolff, yet I was delighted to read some of the same words I'd read in the comic:

And held each other.
—for a couple of days.

Yep, still gets me all verklempt. Chip and Dennis are from such very different walks of life. "Common wisdom" tells you that that kind of relationship can never work. Apparently, in this case, common wisdom has its head up its ass.

The five chatty and compelling long letters were written during the years 1988 to 1991, to Robert Bravard, Kate Spencer and Erin McGraw. Chip talks frankly about life and teaching and falling in love, moments of sadness, moments of joy, world affairs; the kind of stuff you'd expect from letters. He also discusses opera, the theatre, and cuisine, reminding me what a Renaissance man he is. They all feature his delightful habit in his writing of folding into the narrative sensory specifics of his surroundings; the ambient temperature and sounds, someone making coffee, etc. The second strong impression I came away with—it's one I've had before—is how generously Samuel R. Delany shares the realness of his life with his audience. It is a great gift to those of us who encounter him. When I was an emerging writer, I was desperately afraid that to have my work published would be to call down upon my head massed disapproval from certain communities of mine which default to heteronormativity. But I developed a tonic against the fear. Whenever timidity made me reluctant to put fingers to keyboard, especially when I was writing explicitly about queerness, sex, and sexuality, not to mention alternative relationship structures and their intersections with race and gender, I would half-humorously ask myself, "What would Chip Delany do?" From reading Chip's bold, frequently transgressive fiction which explores similar topics, I felt I already knew the answer. But simply asking the question in those circumstances would shore up my faltering boldness. I'd be able to let the words out of my head and commit them to paper without shame. For that, Chip, and for so many other things, my deepest gratitude.

LETTERS FROM AMHERST

1

TO ROBERT BRAVARD
February 21, 1989

• • •

Dept. of Comp. Lit.
South College Building
U. of Mass., Amherst
Amherst MA 01003
February 21, 1989

Dear Bob,

Well, here I am — at last with a little time to write.

Spent the morning at home, making out checks for $316.89 worth of bills. At the cafe on the corner, ran into our department's junior-faculty-genius, Peter Fenves. At 28, he's a respected and widely published Kantian and deep into a book on Kierkegaard. One of my graduate students, a 31-year-old Lesbian named Mel, with peach-colored hair, a couple of years his senior, said of him recently: "It's really nice to have someone on the faculty who actually *lives* in ancient Greece." Peter's dark, skinny, bespectacled, tiny-fingered, distracted, curly-haired, delicately opinionated, and very good-hearted. Mel's description is pretty accurate — though Peter's Greece probably grants Walter Benjamin and Hölderlin honorary citizenship. He came here the same time I did, from Johns Hopkins. I'm in the midst of reading an article he published last year on George Eliot's first book, *Scenes of Clerical Life*. Writing a bit clunky, but content fine.

Eliot's monster, Dempster, is Peter's antihero — because Dempster tells perfectly absurd and baseless stories and insistently sticks to them in the face of truth, the French encyclopedia, common sense, and everything!

A couple of nights ago, I took him and Don Levine (another professor) to dinner, and we'd yakked about Proust and *Madame Bovary* and modernism and drank Irish coffees till two in the morning in the lounge of a place whose name I can't remember. Apparently a comment I dropped that evening sent him home to reread *Hiawatha* (I found out this morning). So we discussed boredom in poetry, in a most unboring fashion, in the crowded restaurant, while I drank decaf and he had coffee.

Then I bundled into my winter coat, while Peter went off to collect his laundry down the road.

Now I'm sitting in my university office on some mid-February holiday — I'm not even sure which one it is. The squirrels are running over the roof. Creatures whose identity I don't want to speculate on rattle around in the walls. And the hallway outside my office is more or less deserted.

My classes are notably better this than last term. I guess people are beginning to hear I'm here — maybe some of last term's students actually talked. At any rate, this time classes were preceded by half-a-dozen calls from particularly interested students who wanted to study with me. In general, the ambition and intelligence — and energy level! — of the classes is so much higher. Last term, though opened to graduate students, my modernist novel class (513) attracted only juniors and seniors. This term, I've got half a dozen graduate students. And the undergraduates who've enrolled seem a lot more *there*.

It's strange to think that I'm here, already sunk in the second term of the rest of my life; the first was, if I'm honest, grim; though — as I look back — not grim in any surprising ways. Half of it was (as I knew it would be) just that the landscape was so new.

By "landscape" I mean something more complex than the physical layout of the town, with its central graveyard [around which my end of Amherst is built], or of the U. Mass. campus, ten minutes down the road from my house. But the bureaucratic landscape, coupled with the psychological landscape [and the social landscape on top of that — the place, as best I can figure out, doesn't *have* a sexual landscape (at least not so's you'd notice)] — has just been annoying, irritating, maddening to learn my way around in. But how could it be otherwise for someone who's spent thirty years basically self-employed in NYC?

My 2nd floor apartment on Cowles Lane is still bare enough to make (my very rare) visitors, when they come in, look about a bit askance.

There's a bed in the main room. A large study table and a couple of benches are almost lost in the front room.

No rugs. No wall decorations. No other objects to speak of—oh, yes: three mismatching kitchen chairs[1] move desultorily through the four low-ceilinged rooms. But that's it. Books are worming their way along the baseboards, having overflowed the two built-in bookshelves.

Still, when I got back after intersession in New York, I actually had a surge of good feeling over the town; coming in my front door, I felt I was coming home. (Thank the Lord, since, for better or worse, it's going to *be* home awhile.)

My office is only a little more homey than the apartment; but because the office has the word-processor in it, I spend most of my days here. One particular "landscape" absurdity is that, though I'm constantly being assigned jobs in which I have to contact other scholars out of state, my phone is *not* set up to make long-distance calls!

Why you'd give a 70-thousand-dollar-a-year distinguished professor a phone that can *only* make local calls inside the Amherst city limits is beyond me! I volunteered to have my own put in that I would pay for completely on my own.

No, said the university.

They like it this way.

Oh, well.

Bob, of late I haven't been the correspondent I'd have liked to be. That goes for a couple of years, now. Looking back over things, I despair of how much has never made it into my letters. You probably noticed "Charles Solomon Coup" on the dedication page of *The Motion of Light in Water*. I met him back in '87; he was a six-three, 26-year-old street kid, somewhat retarded, with a couple of stints in jail for not much of anything, who hailed from Western Pennsylvania's hills, and with whom I had a pleasant summer-long affair that year, which straggled on and off over a year more. Once Iva came home from summer camp and the main part of Mike's and my relation subsided (by mutual consent) into occasional visits (with friendly sex, if Iva was at her mother's), a few months later he more or less settled in with another lover, a pleasant,

---

1. Lent to SRD by SF writer and translator for the deaf Geary Gravel.

hyper-talkative Puerto Rican artist in his thirties named Paul. Though the last time Mike and I ended up in bed together (Mike is Charles's street name. In fact it's "Mike Smith," yes, after the Heinlein hero in *Stranger in a Stranger Land*: Mike can't read, but someone out on the street gave it to him when he first got to the city; so he kept it) was the first time I came down to the city, after I started up here. And of course he's twenty-eight or nine, now. I've had Mike and Paul over for dinner a couple of times, and—when the two of them were kicked out of Paul's Brooklyn flat—I put them up for a few days.

I met Charles/Mike while he was sitting on the rim of a trash can, in front of the Burger King out on Broadway, about a week after my mother's 2nd of July stroke. After drinking a couple of cans of beer together, on the bench in the island in the middle of Broadway, over a few nights, when I'd run into him in the street after I'd come from St. Vincent's, and buying him a couple of Chinese take-out meals, one Sunday I found him in Riverside Park, during the sweltering New York summer heat. (He was standing by the large stone newel, just inside the 79th Street entrance, and looking a little confused about where to amble on to next.) Finally I asked him how he'd take to bedding down with me. He (a nail-biter to rival John Mueller) grinned and said: "That'd be okay. It don't bother me none. I done that before." Later, when we got to know each other better, he told me that the reason he'd first gone along with it was because I'd mentioned I had an air conditioner. At any rate, by the next day, this six-foot-three, size-thirteen-sneakered, easygoing hillbilly who *really* likes to get his tits sucked ("It's funny, but nobody ever does that enough. Men or women. I like gettin' my tits sucked almost more'n my dick. You suck on them for me, and I'll do *anything* for you, man —anything!") had basically moved in.

At fifteen, Mike was tested at school (in which, after staying back for two years, he still couldn't read) and diagnosed as a "slow learner" and "borderline retarded." It precipitated a kind of a family crisis: an older sister threw a tantrum and declared she ". . . didn't want no retard for a brother!" Mike went out into the woods and, rather ineffectually, tried to commit suicide. But it didn't work—or he couldn't do it. He slunk back home. His parents (who had five other kids) were just bewildered and not too sure what to do. But Mike's growing estrangement from the family started about then—though once a week, he still calls his mother.

I don't know if either one of us really found the other's company too stimulating. When he talks, Mike's conversation is pretty limited to the guns he would like to have owned but couldn't afford, the crimes he would like to have committed but never had the guts to do. Once I took him to an SF party given by some fans (Computer engineer and executive secretary wife) over on West End Avenue. Mike had a perfectly fine time. Shyness is not his problem. But when it was time to go home and I went to collect him, he'd got some bespectacled law student in the kitchen corner by the icebox and, with a beer in one hand, was affably and unwittingly terrorizing the young man with his easy and endless recitation of these only just-never-quite-accomplished deeds of violence. (Mike is very large, with a kind of scraggly beard—and, because his hair is thinning, almost never takes his baseball cap off.) As I took Mike's arm and, with a tug, told him, "Hey there, big guy! It's time for us to go home and let these people go to sleep!" the young man blinked at me above the brown knot of his tie between the forest green tabs of his collar and said, "You have a . . . very interesting friend, Mr. Delany."

But *I* certainly found the friendship comforting, especially while I was going through the first months with my mother. And, even after he'd officially "moved out" on the last weekend of August, from the way he'd occasionally drop by and crawl into bed with me, probably he did too —since I'm always willing to listen to him. And not a lot of people are.

Over a very rough period, he was one of the major people who got me through that very hard time. He really deserves his dedication.

You probably got a couple of stories from me about Danny McLaughlin. (Another dedicatee of the book.) But there are many, many more —Danny is currently in jail up in Ontario.

And John Mueller, who got out of jail last February, after finally getting fired for the last time from his machine shop job in New Rochelle, went on a drunken toot about three months ago that ended him up in Florida—where he was shortly picked up. Because he'd broken parole, he's back in jail, this time in Sing-Sing. Got a letter from him only three days ago.

Nor do you know anything about Maison Bailey, a tree-service worker,

[5]

with a surgically corrected harelip, who lives in Brewster, New York, and whom I've been seeing on and off since last April. Maison is (incidentally) the single person I've been most in love with in my life. Bar none. Ever. Alas, the relation is down to twice a week phone calls, now that I'm up here.

My good friend John (Del Gaizo, whom I jokingly call "Big Del Gaizo Fellow") has been going with SF writer (my fellow *Little Magazine* editor and former student from the Clarion SF Writers' Workshop) Susan Palwick, for six months now. I hope it lasts. Because the two of them are about my all-time favorite people. John, the most patient of heterosexual men, has had to hold my hand and listen for what must be days' worth of hours now, to the intricacies of the Maison affair: John is the only one of my New York friends actually to *meet* Maison!

At some point, I really will have to tell you about him. But because it's the relation that's meant most to me since I was a kid, it'll have to wait for a letter all its own.

Through all the last couple of years, Barbara Wise has been a wonderfully fine friend. I spent a couple of weeks with her and Howard up on the Cape last summer. (Howard is failing fast. I don't expect him to last out the year.) But this past spring, Barbara, Big Del Gaizo Fellow, and I all acted in a production of Ionesco's *Jack, or the Submission*, directed by Cynthia Belgrave, out at her basement CBA Theater on Bergen Street in Brooklyn. I played Father Jack. Barbara was Mother Jack. And John was Father Robert. (The leads—Jack and Roberta—were taken by a totally impossible and wonderfully handsome black Jamaican actor, Donald Lee Taylor, and a wonderfully talented actress, Bette Carlson.) There's a videotape of the entire production on store at the Mugar Memorial Library at Boston. And one or two of the SF crowd (Debbie Notkin and Ellen Kushner) actually got out to see it.

Barbara's come up to Amherst a couple of times to visit. Her stepson, Jeremy, lives in town. Barbara and I had an absurd adventure here one night, back in early December, when she and I had gone dancing at a local Amherst nightspot, the Pink Cadillac. It ended up with Barbara running a red light in town, getting arrested, and spending a night in jail in Belchertown—while I and another friend, Mackie, ran all over

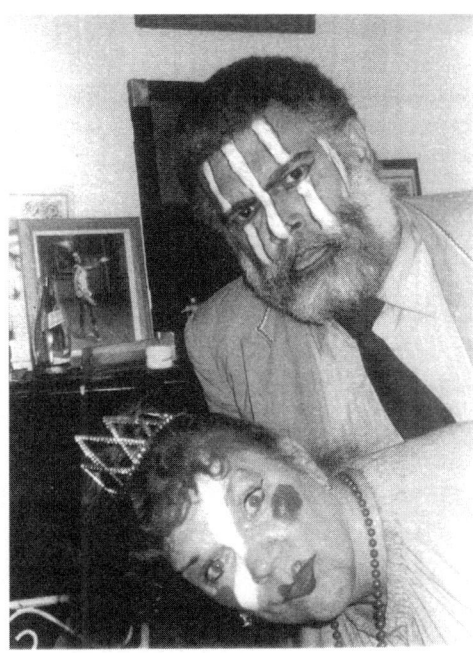

Chip Delany and Barbara Wise as Father Jack and Mother Jack in Eugène Ionesco's Jack, or The Submission, *upstairs in the changing area of Cynthia Belgrave's CBA Theater, April 1988.*

Chip Delany & Barbara Wise as
Father Jack and Mother Jack, April '88

Amherst, trying to keep all this from Jeremy and the rest of the family, who consider Barbara just *a bit* wild anyway.

I spent the six weeks from Christmas till the start of classes (Feb. 1st) down in New York with Iva. We had great fun.

She's happily ensconced at the Bronx High School of Science and doing well. All Christmas Eve I found myself wondering about and thinking of you. It seems on so many other Christmas Eves I've somehow been able to find the time to sit down and write you. And three weeks later, on Iva's birthday, I found myself getting all ready to write you yet again, as I've done so many years now. But this year, for the first time, Iva decided she didn't want to have a party. So, instead of the burst of cleaning in the morning, with the rest of the day free while the kids entertained each other, she and I spent the whole day together. And *another* letter didn't get written — though she and I had a wonderful time.

Toward the end of January, down from Canada and on her way to Montego Bay, Judith Merril stopped off to stay with Iva and me for three very nice days. It was quite wonderful to have a house guest. For one thing, if just for those three days, it got me into regular cooking — we had beef stew the night of Judy's arrival, and I made real breakfasts in the morning. Indeed, on the evening of the second night, Judy said, "Chip, what is the fanciest thing you can do with breakfast eggs?"

Working at the dining room table on the manuscript for the English edition of *Motion of Light in Water*, I looked up and frowned. "I don't know. You can sheer them, I suppose. Then there's eggs Florentine, poached over fresh spinach — that's nice. And of course you can always fall back on Benedict. Why do you ask?"

"Because tomorrow's my birthday," Judy said. "And I'm only going to be here for breakfast. And I'd like some birthday eggs."

"You shouldn't have told him that!" Ending a telephone conversation in the corner, Iva laughed. She stood up from the maroon chair. "Now he'll be off to Zabar's for all sorts of stuff — and knowing how *he* cooks, he would have started this morning if you let him, so that there'd be things fresh baked for tomorrow!"

"I know how he cooks, too," Judy said. "That's why I waited till ten o'clock at night to tell him. So he *couldn't* take too much trouble. Really, eggs will do."

But of course I dashed out (without letting Judy know) and managed to sneak some champagne back into the house. And since Judy tends to sleep late (and Zabar's opens at 8:00 in the morning), I was over getting smoked salmon and sable and watercress (and fresh hot bagels from H&H—Judy had been going on about how she so missed good New York deli food), with scarf wound round my nose, against the January chill.

The eggs themselves were simply scrambled in a double boiler with butter, fresh chives, and a dash of Worcestershire. But the fish and bagel and champagne accoutrements were something.

We sat down to the table at nine-thirty and "breakfasted" till noon.

Iva was at her most mature and charming—finally to go off to a Saturday morning baby-sitting job towards eleven.

Judy left from breakfast, an hour after Iva, to go meet Tom Disch for lunch.

It was all quite fun.

Now one of Judy's reasons for coming down through New York was that her grandson, Kevin, at twenty-four, was expecting his first child. The last time I'd seen Kevin was well over a dozen years ago, when I'd visited his mother, Merril, in Milford PA, back when Kevin was a rambunctious moppet of eight. Judy had timed her trip through the city on the off chance it would take in the new baby's birth and she might drop down to Philadelphia to see them. ("But it's their first kid, and first children are always two weeks late. So I don't really have much hope.") Sure enough, however, twenty minutes after she'd left to meet Tom, there was a phone call from a very tired and precise sounding young man: "Is Judith Merril there . . . ?"

"I'm sorry," I said. "She just left for lunch. You missed her by about twenty minutes."

"Well," he said. "This is her grandson, Kevin. Could you please give her a message for me. Now be sure she gets it exactly: 'Happy Birthday, Great Grandma!'"

Well, of course I exploded with congratulations and good wishes (and the obligatory, "I know you don't remember me, Kevin, but the last time I saw *you* was . . ."), then had a chat with Merril, his mom, who was there. And whom I hadn't talked to for a decade. (The last time I

DELANY / LETTERS FROM AMHERST

actually saw *her* was when she came to New York and picked me up at the Heavenly Breakfast, to drive me down to Milford, and we had an interesting encounter with some high school drop-out toughs in a diner where we'd stopped for coffee. One came up to me in what was clearly an attempt to start trouble and asked: "Hey, fella. Who does your hair?" —as it was all over my head in a very long proto-Afro [also I wore an earring at the time, back then when everybody else didn't], the part that wasn't in a very bushy ponytail.

(In perfect innocence I answered, 'Oh, I do it myself,' and went back to my coffee, while Merril—who was rather heavy and more familiar than I with the mores of the area—held her breath on the counter stool beside me, waiting for the first punch . . . which never flew. Because it never occurred to me that the guy with the denim jacket, pimply chin, open sweatshirt, and the tattoos showing over his t-shirt collar wasn't *perfectly* serious. Back in the car Merril and I laughed about it for the rest of the trip down.) At any rate, Judy's new (and first), great-grandchild was a girl, five-and-a-half pounds, named Kelly Nichole. Mother and daughter were both fine. (It's quite astonishing to think of Merril, who's only a couple of years older than I am, as a grandmother!) And when I got off the phone, I called Tom, who hadn't left to meet Judy yet, and conveyed the message. "Now be sure to get it right," I said. "'Happy Birthday, Great Grandma!'"

As pleased as I was, Tom assured me he would.

That evening when she came in, Judy filled me in on the *rest* of the story. Tom had waited till she was seated at the restaurant table before he'd reached across, taken her hand, and given her the message. The waitress had just come up to take their order, and overheard it.

So when desert time came, she brought two, both with candles, and the whole restaurant sang Happy Birthday. Twice. Telling me all this, Judy sat back on the couch, laughing. "It was really the most wonderful 67th birthday present anyone could *possibly* have!"

Over a couple of gossip sessions Judy told me things about her life—and the SF world—that were just fascinating. In this tiny circle in which I've made my living for so many years, much of the gossip about Judy has the quality of legend already. And the first evening she was there, David Hartwell and Kathryn Cramer came over—and David tried, not very subtly, to prompt her into writing an autobiography; an idea she likes, I think. If she does it, it will be quite wonderful for any of us sunk in the field's mythology.

She told us about her early affair with the legendary John Michel, a Futurean who never really wrote any SF but who was the acknowledged genius of the bunch, the mentor of Pohl and Kornbluth and Asimov as well as of Judy. ("My first half-dozen sales—mysteries and westerns, all—were just a case of writing down what John told us to write. Then revising them the way he told us to revise them. It was pretty much the same with Fred and Ike too, I guess.") She told us the perfectly hysterical story of how Donald Wollheim finally told Michel that he could no longer see Judy because she had been a Trotskyite (Wollheim was a Stalinist; none of them were over twenty-one) and tried to expel her from the group; and how she and Virginia Kidd had gotten the rest of them together and expelled *them* from the Futureans in return.

"Where was Sam Moskowitz in all this?" I asked.

Judy laughed. "Off in New Jersey, I suppose, writing *The Immortal Storm.*"

She told us about her first meeting with Ted Sturgeon, who was rooming down the street from her with Jay Stanton at the time in the late '40s when her Fuller Brush Man informed her that there was an SF writer living in the neighborhood—and Judy, already a Sturgeon fan, sent Ted a fan letter and was invited to come over.

She also spoke of her equally legendary affair with Walter O. ("Darfsteller," *Canticle for Leibowitz*) Miller, from half a dozen years later. And how, with their combined five children, they fled about the country, now to Texas, now to Chicago, now to Florida, to escape hounding X-es. ("For better or for worse, it really was the passion of my life. I remember once, in some hotel, we were in bed together. And in the dark, after we'd just finished making love, Walt said to me: 'We're both wonderful performers. And we've both found the perfect audience. I wonder if we'll ever perform for anyone else?' But really, that was the level the whole thing happened on—" she chuckled, sitting back on the green couch Big Del Gaizo Fellow had given me the month before, raising the general designer standard of the living room by a good three-hundred percent—"or almost all of it, anyway.") In the course of the story, she

[11]

recounted a harrowing scene, when, in some shack in Florida, long, lanky Fred Pohl showed up to physically wrest back his and Judy's mutual daughter, Ann, at which point Walt came in with a gun. ("Fred, with impressive bravery—he really *didn't* know it wasn't loaded—grabbed the thing by the barrel and yanked it out of Walt's hands!") The two men ended up rolling all over the kitchen floor (". . . while I stood there like a ninny, crying, 'You can't *do* that in here! If you're going to do that, take it *outside*! Go on, don't fight in here! Fight outside'"). Fred's glasses got broken. ("That was really the end of it, because without them he was perfectly blind—only Walt didn't know *that*!") Three-year-old Merril came running up to her 26-year-old ex-stepfather with all the fragments—Fred was still searching around for them on the floor—and said: 'Here they are, daddy!'"

The story went on, tense with out-of-state phone calls and advice from Milt Amgott (up until half a dozen years ago my own aging lawyer, but back in the late-'40s the entire science fiction community's legal eagle), and climaxed in the custody trial at which Judy lost Ann to Fred and at which, quite to Judy's astonishment, Walt's refined, southern Gentle Woman mother testified on Judy's behalf. ("Ah can think of no home in which Ah would prefer to see my grandchildren raised.") I was impressed, Judy told me. The judge was impressed. But then, Mrs. Miller was a very impressive woman!

Still, the verdict went against Judy—since it was nineteen fifty and she and Walt were unquestionably "living in sin"; also Fred had now married Carol, and thus had an unstained home for the kids to come to.

That custody trial polarized the whole SF community. It is actually the explanation—I've known this for years—for the perfectly mindless selection of SF writers cited in Kingsley Amis's *New Maps of Hell*. (Only the Pohl-side writers are represented in the book.) And although Fred and Judy have more or less healed their breach and appear on panels with each other and are probably, today, a bit more friendly than M. and I (I have even seen them dance together at an SF convention party!), you can still see the traces of the alignments in the attitudes of the older writers, even today.

The day Judy left for the Caribbean, Barbara Wise's 25-year-old daughter, Julie, got married in a truly sumptuous home wedding. For the affair, I actually bought my first pair of dress shoes in about ten years. Then, a trip to the thrift store on 98th Street netted me a Pierre Cardin suit that *almost* fits, for a mere thirty dollars. It's really quite handsome. Iva picked up her best party clothes from her mother's, then she and I went down to attend on Sunday evening. I wept through the whole service, while Iva giggled at me.

The one real sadness there was that Barbara's close friend Michael had been supposed to help out tending bar. I think I mentioned to you that he had AIDS, when we all had Christmas dinner together at Barbara's in '87. Well, the day of the wedding, he had to go into the hospital; he's been falling a lot, sleeping even more; and a cat scan shows it's gone to the brain — which is how it took Ralph, the year before. This may well be it. But the ceremony was lovely.

The bride looked beautiful. A harpist and flautist played throughout. All of Howard's electronic art was a-glitter, a-flash, and a-blink about their sepulchrally large living room — including the great, John Ray wall light-sculpture (which had been on the fritz for the last half dozen years, but which Barbara had gotten Ray in to fix for the occasion — *he* lives here in Amherst, too! Barbara and I spent a lovely evening with him in December). The food Barbara managed to get together (down in the well that drops through the midst of the living room floor stood an immense ice sculpture of a dragon, set about with spring tropic flowers — because the newlyweds were to be honeymooning in the tropics) was beyond belief:

Shrimp. Ham. Vegetarian crepes. New potatoes stuffed with caviar (Sevruga!), salads and wonderfully fresh vegetables, and three kinds of champagne for the various courses — Deutch with the canapés, Taittinger with the entree — and (a daring move that worked, just taking people's heads off!) *peach* champagne with the sumptuous wedding cake.

I had a long talk with one of the groom's 17-year-old sons, and decided that — though going through a rough adolescence — he is a profoundly good kid.

There were about a hundred guests.

This Christmas my sister had given us tickets to Andrew Lloyd (*Jesus Christ Superstar, Evita, Cats, Starlight Express*) Webber's and Charles Hart's *The Phantom of the Opera.*

The Monday after the wedding, on January 23rd, wearing much what we'd worn the night before, Iva and I went to see it.

It's customary to say that the show is dreadful — but it's just musically rather complicated. The production is lavish (and the season's hugest Broadway success) on an order that the Broadway term "lavish" doesn't usually cover. As spectacle, it makes it almost impossible to pay attention to the music — which is a decent modern-middlebrow *leitmotif* opera. But the spectacle is, I'm sure, why it's successful.

The opening twin scenes *are* breathtaking. You enter a theater in ruins, with scenery fallen over the stage and gray hangings covering the proscenium, dust cloths on all the scenic statuary, some of which shows, broken and tarnished, from beneath it.

The lights go down, and, on stage, an auction starts. Objects from the old theater are being sold off. An old man in a wheelchair buys a little music box, on which a figure of a monkey plays cymbals. Lying askew on the stage, a huge, old theatrical chandelier is uncovered. The auctioneer explains that this is, indeed, the chandelier that figured in the disaster involved with "the strange affair of the Phantom of the Opera, never fully explained." An attempt to illuminate the old object produces a sudden shower of sparks and short circuits, but suddenly the cables begin to haul the clinking, glittering object up from the boards, out over the audience, and toward the actual theater ceiling — at which point the entire *house* (not just the stage), over some twenty-eight bars of thunderous triple-*fff* organ, mostly in darkness, but with shafts of light darting now here, now there, to spotlight some instant of the transformation, returns to its 1890's gilt and gaslit splendor!

It all settles down on a moment when a sort of clunky but colorful Meyerbeer-style opera (*Hannibal*?) is in progress on the stage.

It's so impressive visually (as is, indeed, the rest of the show, with its underground lakes of dry ice, its disappearing mirror walls, its tilting subterranean stairways), you can't possibly concentrate on the fairly intricate — and modestly intelligent — musical development.

I've been listening to the tapes, though, and I've ascertained that there really is *something* (if not *that* much) going on.

I read Gaston Leroux's novel a couple of months back, before I saw the show. John Del Gaizo was a loader and workman at the Beacon

Theater, which they revamped for the opening-night cast party. John's stories from *that* evening are a tale in themselves! The novel is a hopelessly clunky mess. Leroux probably wrote it for three-part serialization in some French monthly pulp—likely without reading the earlier installments when working on the latter ones.

In the book, there're really *three* phantoms (one of which, the mysterious rat-catcher in the theater cellar, was clearly going to get some sort of story to himself, before he got abandoned as Leroux came closer to the end), and heaven alone knows what Leroux thought *the* ending was going to be when he began—clearly he didn't want to close off *any* possibilities! I'm sure when he started out, the mysterious Turk who is always wandering around back stage (and who turns out, quite unexpectedly, to be a detective, who takes the callow young hero, Raoul, under his wing and proceeds to solve the mystery) was going to turn into the first Phantom. But G.L. probably decided that was too obvious. Eric (the Phantom we all know and love) must have more professions (engineer, architect, composer, singing teacher, magician, sideshow manager, assassin, oriental torturer, horse trainer . . .) than any other character ever to make it through a penny-dreadful. All of which professions he's superb at—of course.

What *is* fascinating however: the book symbolizes beautifully the uncomfortable psychological underside of the transformation of the early 19th century, perpetually lit-up romantic theater of light into the late romantic, Wagnerian theater of darkness. The whole creaky melodrama is a black and reactionary allegory of the transformation that accompanies it, not only in the performing arts, but in all the rest as well, between early "performer-as-craftsman," socially only a little higher than a prostitute, and "performer-as-artist" (truly concerned about the work, obsessive over study and the spiritual center of the music, possessed by the artist and his mission) that accompanied the theatrical transformation Bayreuth brought about in the general art world between 1876 and the death of Edward VII in 1910 (the year of *The Phantom*'s first book publication). For most of the original story, the Phantom is not real. He is only in Christine's mind. But at the same time he is her singing teacher and the composer of the new and supremely difficult opera that all the traditional singers find nearly impossible to learn their parts in . . .

[15]

It really is a straight portrayal of the Wagner mythos.

The chandelier the Phantom brings crashing down mid-story on the audience, murdering one unfortunate woman in the stalls, is doubtless an old-fashioned gas or candle-lit affair, which burned under the ceiling of the theater throughout the performance. The new one that goes up to replace it (and which the new theater managers are so proud of) is certainly an electric one, which is extinguished during performances — rendering the theater dark (and modern!), à la Bayreuth, but which — problematically and allegorically — allows the Phantom an even *easier* time in wreaking his murderous mischief on all and sundry.

Note that more than half the Phantom's actual energy is directed toward the two new Paris Opera managers on "how his theater is to be run" and securing his 20-thousand-francs-per-quarter salary! I mean, how Wagnerian could you get? The Webber show, incidentally, takes it out of the Paris Opera and replaces it in an imaginary theater called The Opéra Populaire.

And — with its "music of the night" theme running through — the B'way show (at any rate) makes a nice, but probably unconscious, nod to Novalis, who supplied both Wagner (*Tristan*, Act II) and all after him with the dark metaphors in which such tales of shadowy obsession traditionally are couched. (*Hymnen an die Nacht.*)

It occurs to me that the original mythologic/historic basis for *The Phantom of the Opera* is quite probably the death of Von Carolsfeld, Wagner's first, twenty-five-year-old Tristan. The Munich Opera had already made *Tristan und Isolde* a thing of gossip, well before its first performance, by abandoning it after an untoward fifty-odd rehearsals, even after the music had already been published and various children, such as Nietzsche [fifteen at the time] and King Ludwig [Prince back then], were playing it on their pianos and waiting on pins and needles for an actual performance.

Six weeks after the actual, first, 1866, royal command performance of the legendarily "unperformable" opera, Von Carolsfeld, devoted to Wagner, died, presumably of typhus, the fever exacerbated during the opera's brief, royal run (that young King Ludwig had finally commanded in the notoriously cold and draughty wings, where, dripping with sweat after the exertions of Act II, Von Carolsfeld had to lie in the cold (though it *was* June), waiting for the even more taxing demands of Act III. Von Carolsfeld (Ludwig Schnorr) died raving, believing he was Tristan and calling for Wagner to heal him. (The rather horrid symptoms of his very unpleasant death make it sound more like a case of galloping syphilis. And Wagner and Cosima were both distraught.) But theater gossip was that there'd been some sexual relationship between the rather heavy, hard-working young tenor (probably not true, since Von Carolsfeld's wife, Malvina, who played Isolde in the same production, was equally devoted to Wagner. But that just made it stranger). One of the reasons for the sexual rumor, however, was that before general rehearsals had begun, the difficulty of the part had obliged Wagner to spend some weeks closeted alone with the young man (whose voice was wonderful and whose enthusiasm was boundless — but whose sight-reading left something to be desired), working with him on the difficult chromaticisms of the Herculeanly taxing part — a most unusual practice that only added to the mythos when, a month and a half later, he died so unexpectedly and unpleasantly.

But, displaced onto a woman, this is probably the Ur-version behind both *The Phantom* and *its* Ur-version, George du Maurier's melodrama *Trilby* (1894).

But little or none of that makes it into the Broadway show.

At any rate, when the music of the night finally got over with, and the lovers were safely off together, and the Phantom had done his last and poignant disappearing act, and we were squeezing up the crowded theater aisle, over the red carpet and between the maroon seats, my daughter (from the height of her new, week-old fifteen years of maturity) told me: "You know, I think Raoul was . . . well, just a pain. She *should* have gone off with the Phantom."

I laughed. "Well, that's what they wanted you to feel. So I guess the show was a success . . . ?"

"It was okay," she allowed, as the first cool air from outside finally reached us over the crowd ahead, squeezing before us, around us, into the lobby. "It was sort of silly, though. The story, I mean . . . I mean, every time stupid, dumb Raoul came on, I just wanted to scream!"

Then there was only squeezing; and no more talking for a while. But as we hurried up 44th Street toward Eighth Avenue, looking for a midnight cab, I wondered how to explain to Iva that, in historical/allegorical terms, Christine really *had* gone off with the dangerous, obsessive Phantom, and not with shallow, reactionary Raoul after all. If you take the Phantom as a demonized symbol for the Wagnerian concept of the artist, fighting for possession of Christine's soul, then, really, in terms of modernist history, things had worked out exactly as Iva'd wished. And the single line of show music, which, that night, was all I'd managed to retain once the curtain had come down, kept playing through my mind, with all its Oedipal edge a-glitter, as Iva and I moved past the theater posters in their glass frames along the wall of the Milford Plaza; "He's here, the Phantom of the Opera . . . I am the Phantom of the Opera . . . !"

A couple of days later I recreated Judy's birthday breakfast for John Del Gaizo. (Iva: "How come we're doing everything so fancy, these days?" Me: "Oh, I don't know. I just feel like it." Iva: "Me too! Me too —don't stop. Could I have some more smoked salmon?" Which tickled Big Del Gaizo Fellow, who had another glass of champagne.) Then, a few days later, while in the nest of my office I worked maniacally at finishing up the last section of the *Camera Obscura* interview for Constance Penley and Sharon Willis (which interview I'm *quite* proud of!), John came up and packed stuff for me—a twenty-five pound box of journals and manuscripts to be Federal Expressed up to Boston and a hundred-twenty-five pound box of books/clothes/cooking utensils/general-stuff for me in Amherst.

Then Iva and Bumper (the cat) went back to Iva's mother's, and the next morning I went down to the bus below Grand Central, rode out to La Guardia, then flew to Erie, Pennsylvania, to deliver a cut-down version of my "Introduction to Deconstruction" lecture[2] for the Mercyhurst College "academic celebration." It went over pretty well—and I kind of fell in love with the blue-collar town.

What else? Just the lectures I guess, first off in Lowell, then again,

---

2. "Neither the First Word nor the Last on Deconstruction, Structuralism, Post-structuralism, and Semiotics for SF Readers," in *Shorter Views: Queer Thoughts and the Politics of the Paraliterary,* by Samuel R. Delany (Hanover, NH: University Press of New England for Wesleyan University Press, 1999).

last weekend, in Philadelphia at the meeting of the Associated Writing Programs of America—I sent you the booklet. But its dry account of panels and programs masks some interesting happenings. First off, the overall theme was a celebration of Allen Ginsberg. Though I've been in the same room with him a couple of times, and though we have many mutual friends (and once a mutual landlord named Chuck Bergman whom both of us, I believe, were occasionally going to bed with), we've never been introduced.

At the upstairs reception after the Gay/Lesbian Panel, then, I was a bit surprised with the scraggly bearded Professor Ginsberg (he's taken John Ashbery's place as Professor of Poetry in the City University System), in his modest brown suit and tie, came up to me and simply said: "Hello, Delany. How've you been?" then launched into a chat about the Cherry Valley Farm, the Naropa Institute (that he runs with our mutual friend, Anne Waldman), etc.[3] Finally he reached into his canvas shoulder bag and handed me a flyer for a series of readings he was putting on, mostly of black poets.

I give him points.

It looks like quite a program he and Gwendolyn Brooks have put together there.

One of the most pleasant people at the AWP was Honor (*Memoir*) Moore. The first night we were there, after most of the panelists went out to dinner at a very good—but crashingly expensive—Japanese place called, incongruously, "Ziggy's," Honor and I snuck off together to the Hershey Hotel's cabaret, and heard a couple of her old friends from Yale perform some standard show tunes quite brilliantly.

Then we went to a reception for *them*, where the food the hotel supplied was far better than the *hors d'oeuvres* it had gotten together for the school teachers. A lot of old Yale people had shown up for the evening. And in the course of sitting around chatting, I realized I was talking to Rhoda Levine, director of Anthony Davis's *X, The Life and Times of Malcolm X*, which I wrote you about a couple of years back, when I was at

3. A dozen years after Ginsberg's death, SRD would teach at Naropa for fifteen summers in their Summer Writing Program.

Cornell. (I sent you a copy of the interview I did with the composer one Sunday morning at the home of Henry Louis Gates, Jr.).[4]

Mayhaps you remember, while I very much appreciated the music, I *hated* the production. In the course of prodding Ms. Levine, who is a very gutsy, New York/Academic theater person, I got some hair-raising stories *about* the production that certainly put a different light on some of it.

One of the reasons the thing ever *got* to Lincoln Center at all was because it came with an assembled cast of pretty professional singers. But the New York State Theater's stage is huge, and the whole thing had to be revamped for a playing area almost three times the size of any they'd performed on before. And it was assumed that they were also not going to need any rehearsal time to speak of—when what Rhoda actually wanted (she explained to me, as she leaned forward in her purple slacks and purple woolly top) was *at least* a hundred hours—i.e., two weeks—of rehearsal time in the new theater.

Well, when the new opera was booked in, there simply wasn't a 100 hours of rehearsal time available.

The compromise they struck was arrived at rather dramatically. When they'd used up the 30 hours that was all Lincoln Center would give them, they hadn't even started on the third act. So Rhoda went to a pay phone and called Beverly Sills and began to explain: "We've finally decided the way we're going to do it.

"At the end of Act II, we're going to stop the whole opera. Dead in its tracks, Beverly! The cast is going to gather on the stage, and we're going to perform the third act as a cantata—no movement, no actions, just characters stepping out of the chorus and singing. Suddenly the whole performance will simply paralyze into total and complete stasis! It's going to be breathtaking!

"You know as well as I do, Beverly—people have been complaining about the rehearsal time available here for years; the lack of funding, the lack of facilities. Well, *besides* being about the economic oppression

---

4. "Anthony Davis—a Conversation," in *Silent Interviews: On Language, Race, Sex, Science Fiction, and Some Comics*, by Samuel R. Delany (Hanover, NH: University Press of New England for Wesleyan University Press, 1994), 289.

of the American Black, this is also of course a meta-opera . . . about *that*! And what better way to dramatize it? Certainly for the cast, this is really an opera about the oppression of the American opera as a theatrical form. They're singers, and that's what they're *really* concerned about. It's about performance standards. It's about what can and can't be done in the theater today with a serious work because there's no money, no time, and no margins for doing it properly. And *you're* going to have it, right on *your* stage — the audience will be devastated, I promise you! People will be talking about it for years!

"There was," Ms. Levine went on with her story, "absolute silence on the other end of the phone. Finally, Beverly said to me: 'Rhoda, how much time do you need?'

"So I said: 'Oh, I thought about eighty-three hours.' And Beverly said: 'You've got it!'" And Rhoda sat back at the crowded round little hotel table, slapping her knees while we laughed.

I *still* think it was a *thoughtless* production. While she certainly delivers a good anecdote, I think she's a director who has no notion (or possibly experience) of what images will *carry* in a space that size and what images won't. Dramatic stage arrangements that are perfectly acceptable on a 25 foot proscenium for a three-hundred seat house can be simply invisible in a thousand-plus seat hall the size of the three major theater spaces at Lincoln Center.

But I enjoyed her story.

The next day, I had a very pleasant lunch with Richard Howard, Honor Moore, and Peter (*The Idiot Princess of the Last Dynasty*) Klappert, at which Richard told us all about a course he'd taught the previous year, called American Ecstatics: It covered a whole range of people, such as Whitman, Isadora Duncan, and Frank Lloyd Wright. Sounded just fascinating.

At the actual panel, I met an interesting young man, an historian and writer on economics named Walter (*Mortal Splendor*) Mead. My piece — the one I sent you last week — opened the panel.[5] But the real winner among the formal presentations was Allan Gurganus's piece, which, when it's printed, I'll send along. It would be unfair to try and reproduce

5. "Gay Writers / Gay Writing."

it informally, since it was so carefully done. Later, while the informal part was going on, and after I made my point about [Guy] Davenport, Richard threw in that a few months ago he'd been talking to Hugh Kenner on the phone.

Kenner has always been one of Davenport's biggest supporters. But Kenner had been complaining to Richard that he just found the sexual content of Davenport's more recent material "absolutely embarrassing" and simply didn't know how he was supposed to deal with it. Richard pointed out that the whole area of pedophilia really puts people off. And I pointed out that Davenport's characters *never* cross any real, legal line. Nevertheless they stray so close that it becomes that much *more* bothersome—because the line is so clearly in the reader's mind.

Both Allan Gurganus and Marianne Hauser had stressed in their pieces the responsibility of the writer to cross boundaries and write about people other than themselves. Men must try to write from the position of women. Women must try to write from the position of men; rich, poor, and all other boundaries must be breached by the writer of fiction.

I made the point toward the end that, however these boundaries were crossed, we had to remember that these same boundaries represented differences in power relationships. Thus, a man writing from the position of a woman was crossing one power boundary and a woman writing from the point of view of a man was crossing another. Hauser had cited some of the criticism she had received in the forties when she'd written a first person novel as a man. I pointed out that what this criticism had actually meant was: "How dare you, a woman, usurp this particular male field of power." And that a man writing as a woman seldom gets such criticism because the male writer assuming a first-person female persona is moving down the power scale, not up.

On the aisle, toward the back of the ballroom in which all this was going on, a little brown woman in a red tam and bundled up in a lot of orange down coat was nodding intently at just about everything I said.

When the panel was over, a great young bear in glasses and a woolly sweater, with a mass of curly hair caught back in a small ponytail, came running up to the table, put his chin over the edge of the pale blue cloth (spotted now with water between the several microphones and Styrofoam cups), and said: "Mr. Delany, I just wanted to tell you: I've proba-bly read everything you've published. And for years I've always thought you were one of the finest writers in America—and certainly the most underrated one. I'm so glad to get a chance to meet you. May I give you this?" and he handed me a copy of *Mortal Splendor*.

"Thank you," I said. "Eh, what is it . . . ?"

"It's my book," he said.

"Oh!" I said. "Well, thank you very much . . ."

Then said young bear turned around and dashed back off into the crowd.

That afternoon in my room I started reading the nicely printed trade paperback with the rather impressive encomiums on the back.

Fifty pages on, and I'd realized that (one) it was quite well written and (two) it was even better in its thinking. It's an analysis of the "Amer-ican Empire" with an extremely cogent set of suggestions on what the country might do to get it together.

The last program of the day was a reading with novelist Toby Olson and poet Sonia Sanchez. Olson is a six-foot-ten bearded, white-blond woodsman of a fellow (I exaggerate, but not by much). He was always at the center of an entourage—and seemed very much into himself. A cou-ple of times I addressed friendly remarks to him, but he never answered. Perhaps because his head is so far above mine, he just didn't hear me.

Alas, I don't much like his work. It's not awful. But it's as sexist and as homophobic as one can get away with these days and still be taken seriously (by those who don't think sexism and homophobia are all *that* serious after all . . .) and I listened to him with a mental blue pencil striking out excess verbal baggage in his prose on a pretty regular basis.

When Sanchez got up to read, I realized she was the brown woman in the orange coat who'd been nodding so enthusiastically in the back of the room during my panel.

Marilyn has mentioned her to me on several occasions—and has apparently arranged readings for her a few times. The mentions were al-ways somewhat mysterious: "Have you ever heard Sonia Sanchez read?"

I'd say no.

And Marilyn would say: "You really should," then go on to talk about something else.

I don't have too much to say about the poems. I suspect they're probably pretty good. Certainly I didn't find myself editing them down the way I had done with Olson's prose. But Sanchez's *performance* was stunning.

First off, I use "performance" not in the sense of drama, but rather in the sense of the way poetry—not theater—*should* be performed. And I don't mean that she was at all restrained. The energy level was jaw-dropping and electric. And, between the poems, she became a kind of political David Antin. She chanted the intra-poetic material at such a level that it almost came out stronger than the poems. Her message is straight Dickens:

Love one another, and we'll all make the world a better place.

But it's a nice one. And I think everyone left the ballroom feeling *even* taller than Toby Olson!

Outside in the hall, Toi Derricotte grabbed me by the shoulder and gave me a hug, just bubbling: "Isn't it wonderful that she *exists*, Chip?"

And I had to allow that it was.

But everyone was simply babbling on about how moving she had been.

As I said to Peter Klappert when we found ourselves lingering together outside: "Talk about American *Ecstatics* . . . ! Richard's got a real live one, right here!"

Really, if she ever passes within a hundred miles of you, you must catch her. For someone under twenty-five years old, I wouldn't be surprised if a single reading by Sanchez might change their lives forever.

That evening, when we were all gathered downstairs again, drinking and making friendly, I hunted out the burly Walter, still in jeans and his sweater, and, between buying each other far too many drinks, we got into a very interesting conversation about his work, about mine. The conversation continued through a banquet dinner (which ended in a sing-a-long with Allen Ginsberg and the Fugs ["And all the hills echoèd . . ." I sang into Ed Sanders' mike as he roamed the hundred in the hall], who'd been reconvened by the AWP Program Director to entertain: it was nice to see Ed Sanders again, who's on the Governing Board with me at New York Foundation for the Arts) in a homage to Blake, and on into the party afterwards.

Mr. Mead (Walter) is a very smart 35.

At one point when some of the other panelists had joined us, he explained that, as a political writer, people are just starting to call on him to testify in political hearings. He's gay—and he's wondering whether he should come out publicly or not. The general opinion was that he should probably not rush that, but that we couldn't really advise him till we knew better what exactly his situation was.

Eventually the conversation thinned down again to the two of us. And then I did something that I have never done before at any SF con or academic convention of any sort. I asked him if he'd like to go to bed. He smiled and said: "Oh, I'd like that very much." Then he asked me: "Is it my hands?" (He'd already mentioned that he'd read *everything* I'd ever published.)

I laughed. "No. It's just you. But it's a little odd to meet 50 perfect strangers who are quite so privy to all your sexual particularities."

"I would probably have said something to you, first," he said. "But because I don't bite my nails, I figured you probably wouldn't be interested."

"Come on," I said.

And we had a very pleasant night of it.

The next morning, after he showered, I took him to breakfast in the hotel's overpriced mezzanine restaurant, then sent him off to his train back to whatever university he hails from. He's not Maison Bailey, but it was still very nice.

A couple of hours later, when I was in the waiting room at the 30th Street Station, I struck up a conversation with a black poet also down at the AWP program, named Walter Mosley, who'd gone to U. Mass., and who recommended several restaurants to me in my own neighborhood I'd never heard of before.

The next three issues of the *New York Review of Science Fiction* will see the "Intro to Deconstruction" (my Lowell/Erie lecture) serialized in three parts. It's kind of fun. I'll send on copies, when I get some.

A couple of nights back, I stayed up till all hours reading René Daumal's *Mount Analogue*, its completion interrupted by Daumal's death in 1944. Then I started on his earlier, completed book, *A Night of Serious Drinking*. (My journal says: "Finally—after how many years [finding it first on the shelf in San Francisco's City Lights in '69] — read *Mount An-alogue*.") What an eccentric and interesting little book. A mystical tract almost wholly without God. Only one of the editorially appended notes gives in to a "Being that holds each thing accomplished," residing at the mountain's peak.[6] But even that's only a mountaineer's song, which Daumal finally decided not to include in the book. In its incomplete and fragmentary form, it seems largely of the Novalis / *Heinrich von Ofterdingen* or *Oberman* tradition. Can't think of another book that comes apart *less* into its respective sentences. A good book to read on a day when you've got a hangover [I'd overindulged at dinner the night before.] . . . The novel proper ends, mid-sentence, in the midst of an ecological parable that is eminently completable on the ideational level; and mentally completing it is one of the most seductive pleasures of the text.

I'd recently recommended it to our department professor who specializes in mystical literature, Lucian Miller (who'd never heard of it! Which gives you an idea of the quality of some of these guys); but I thought I'd really better read it myself before I handed it over. It quite lives up to its reputation.

Then, day before yesterday I got a call from Frank — down in New York. He'd gone over to the apartment, checking for mail in the mailbox. (Can you imagine. Three years after our break-up, he's *still* getting mail there!) Because it was kind of stuffed, he took everything out and called me up to find out if I wanted him to read any of it to me over the phone. Among the stuff there was a new copy of the *Australian SF Review*; they just devoted an entire issue to me. He says he's going to get the mail back to the house, but, though I know he has the best intentions, I suspect I'll never actually *see* any of it again. But that's just Frank.

Still, I'd rather like to find out what Russell Blackwell had to say about me. He's really the best critic yet (present company excepted!) who's written about me. Too bad he's down under.

But that more or less brings you up to date.

I wish there was that much to tell you about the work. But I'm not even going to try.

---

6. This, of course, is discourse; though it is not a being, it is a process entailing brains and a world — the ones that *are* the cases (Wittgenstein).

Well, this is about half the letter I should write you! And I have not even started to respond to *your* letters. But I want to get this off, just so you'll know I haven't forgotten you.

Someone is supposed to show up here at ten to start giving me lessons in American Sign Language[7] (which I know a little bit of already), and there is an Undergraduate Studies Committee Meeting at noon. And someone just printed up and distributed a poster for a guest speaker (Henry Sussman), that apparently has the wrong date on it, about which various people are running around and being mildly hysterical.

My love to you and yours.

Really, I *still* owe you a letter in which I actually *answer* yours! (I ought at least to mention that the awful situation with Michael P. is one I've encountered a couple of times in the last year. Larry McCaffery just went through his own version of the same thing, when a young graduate student brought charges of sexual harassment against him [from what I know of both the man and of such situations, it's equally as unlikely as it was in Michael's case] that flowered into something truly unpleasant. I wonder what this is indicative of?) But that will have to wait till the next moment I get some time.

All good thoughts
for more good things,

Samuel R. Delany

---

7. Geary Gravel — see note 1 above.

2

TO ROBERT BRAVARD

May 22, 1990

. . .

21 Cowles Lane
Amherst MA 01002

May 22, 1990

Dear Bob,

Received yours of March 1 / May 17th, and responded pretty much by rereading everything you've sent — back to October 25th, 1989. Though it's entirely my fault, there *are* a few holes in the story I'd like to catch up on. First off: How is Cynthia?

You told me about the beginnings of her knee problem — then, your own hip problem (understandably!) superseded it in your account. Nevertheless, while I have a sense of how you're doing (and it doesn't sound fun!), I'm still concerned whether both or just one of you is currently severely limited in getting around!

We're a handful of days beyond the end of classes. I spent the afternoon writing letters (one form letter, actually, but with a personalized first paragraph) to all the graduate students who'd received Teaching Assistantships, telling them which faculty member each would be working with (if any), and what courses each would be teaching.

I did the personalizing, however, so I might as well have been writing out 12 letters.

I also told our reigning disaster case, a 30-ish young man from Hungary (Rajmund), that the department had decided not to support him this year. Because he's from an eastern bloc country, essentially this means he'll have to drop out of graduate school here. He's been known to have quite a temper — but he likes me, so I'm afraid that, rather than get angry, he just kind of fell apart. The sad thing is, it's not his marks that are the problem — though they are not spectacular. He simply has an appalling attitude toward things intellectual and work in general, which the department has no way to deal with. Fundamentally, he can't conceive that there might be anything worth knowing that he doesn't already know. Thus, when a term or phrase (e.g., "lexia," "contradictory relationship," "irony against both sides") comes up in the professor's lecture that he's not always/already familiar with, instead of going to the professor and asking for some further explanation, he simply dismisses it as academic nonsense not worth bothering about. Then, when the students in his discussion group ask him for explanations of the same terms, he raises his eyes to heaven and declares, "Don't ask me. You'll have to ask Professor Moebius. I have no idea what it means."

A chairman's job is not (always) a happy one. But, as my friend John Del Gaizo (who is subletting my apartment back in the city) keeps reminding me, what they pay you for is the unpleasant parts of your job: failing kids and telling good-hearted disasters that they have to go home.

At this point, though, I must tell you about a pleasant young fellow of 36 whom I've known for most of a year and who has been living with me, here and in the city, for the past two months. His name is Dennis Rickett. For six years he's been homeless and living on the New York streets. His stomping grounds for the past couple of years have been 72nd Street, where he had a blanket full of books he sold from during the day.

One winter's day, when I was down from Amherst for a few days, I went past, when he was squatting at the corner of his book display —a very dirty guy in an even dirtier jump suit, fiddling with a fairly large radio.

A maroon paperback of Norman Podhoretz's *Making It* lay on the ground, and I picked it up. It was priced at two dollars. I decided I wanted to read it, and went digging under my winter coat at my pocket.

But I'd left my wallet at home.

I laughed and told the guy what had happened. Under his woolen cap, pulled low over a few year's growth of gray-shot hair, he smiled over a mouth full of almost no teeth at all within his scraggly, once-red beard and waved a big gray-black hand at me with bitten nails: "Take it. You can bring me the money the next time you come by . . .

So I did.

[29]

("Hey, you really brought it back," he said, with a faintly bemused smile on the slightly warmer Wednesday morning, two days later. "I didn't think you would.")

Which is how I first began talking with Dennis. He was a quiet, good natured, very simple guy. His old man had been an alcoholic truck driver, occasionally in jail, but very close with Dennis. They'd worked together, all through Dennis's adolescence and early twenties. Dennis loved him a lot. One night Dennis was out at a bar. His father, drunk and on foot, went looking for him—was hit by a truck and killed. Dennis's family—none too bright Irish/German working class, from Brooklyn—kept ribbing Dennis about his father's death being Dennis's fault. Dennis started to drink heavily, while carrying on an affair with (in his words) "a fat, nymphomaniac girlfriend," which ended, after two years, with girlfriend gone, Dennis and his family permanently estranged, and Dennis (then age thirty) living on the streets.

With his shopping cart full of books and belongings, he'd been at his present location for about a year—going across Central Park at night to sleep in the doorway of a Madison Avenue art dealer's, then coming back in the morning (stopping in the park's public restroom—when it was open—for minimal washing, to masturbate, and take a dump) to the West Side to sell his books, look out for cars, do little side-walk sweeping up jobs for the store owners around.

For the first three months I knew him, it was the most passing of acquaintances. Then, I began going down to look for him in his doorway and to hang out with him for the odd hour. Sometimes, standing around on the street, we'd have a coffee. Sometimes we'd have a beer. In the course of that time, Dennis got rid of the shopping cart, and began to travel with a backpack—which he wore almost constantly and which must have weighed a good fifty, if not sixty-five, pounds. Oddly, it was Dennis who first brought up the possibility of sex—with a passing quip between beers, back in mid January:

"I got it pretty good out here," he told me one day. "All I really need is a lover." Which he presented as kind of a joke, since he was dirty enough—no, the word I want is filthy—enough to preclude most people's sexual interest in him.

A couple of days later, when we were again talking on a rather blustery winter's day, he shoved his hands deep into his jumpsuit pockets, grinned at me, then looked wistfully off down the street. "You know, I ain't been to bed with a women in six years. You hear women talk about guys who just want to keep them for their bodies, an' they don't like it. Well, I wouldn't mind it if some guy wanted to keep me just for my body. Me, I think it'd be kinda pretty cool."

Both comments stay with me because I didn't respond to either one — at least right away. But a day later, when I went down, I asked Dennis if he was serious what he'd said yesterday. He said,

"Maybe, I don't know," which is what Dennis says to a lot of things — today, I know that that's generally his code for "yes"; but at the time I didn't.

We talked about our mutual sexual preferences — what we did and didn't like to do in bed with other men. We both agreed they sounded pretty complementary. I said that if he was serious, maybe we should try spending a little time together. Yes, I found him attractive, underneath (and, hell, just a bit because of) the dirt. Dennis's response was, "Yeah, maybe we should. We seem to get along pretty good."

I was back and forth from Amherst a couple more times before I put a proposition to him:

"Look," I told him one morning. "I'm going to get a motel room for a couple of days. We can go there, spend some time, and see how things work out."

"You wanna do that?" he asked.

"Yes," I said. "I do."

"Okay."

And the next time I came down, as soon as I got off the bus, I went to the Skyline Motel on 10th Avenue and 49th Street, rented a room for the weekend, and came back to seventy second street that afternoon with the pair of rectangular plastic "keys" (perforations at one end, like single ended dominos), and showed them to him. "I've got a room. You want to keep yours? And you can come down there, whenever you like."

"Naw," he said. "You keep it, for me. I don't wanna go there by myself. I wanna go there together." Generally a pretty indecisive guy, sometimes he's quite straightforward.

So we agreed I would pick him up at nine o'clock that night. One of

Dennis's jobs was watching out for people's illegally parked cars. An owner of a bedding store on the block gave Dennis ten bucks a day to watch his car; if the police came down the block, giving out tickets, Dennis would go into the shop and get him, and the man would drive his car off before the police made it to his spot. "And he don't leave the store, sometimes," Dennis explained to me, "till eight-thirty or nine sometimes."

At nine that night, with a Pakistani cab driver supremely indifferent to my muddled instructions about picking up a friend on 72nd and continuing down to 49th, I took a taxi down to the all but deserted commercial street.

No Dennis.

So I got out and let the cab go, wondering if he'd chickened out. I ambled over to stand in his doorway, thinking I'd give him half an hour to show up. Every five minutes or so, I'd glance up and down the street.

After about ten minutes, I glimpsed a figure wearing a backpack, carrying a bed roll, and hurrying from the east. Through his scraggly beard, Dennis grinned at me. "Oh, man!" he said, hurrying up to me. "I'm glad you're here. I kept thinking I was gonna miss you!"

"I was going to wait," I told him. "It's okay."

"Fifteen minutes to nine," he said, putting down his bed roll, "and I suddenly gotta take a dump in the worst way. I says to myself, oh, no—God, don't do this to me now! But it was one of those that wasn't gonna hold off. So I had to go over to Central Park and find a spot where I could do it."

"You okay now?" I asked him.

"Yeah." He grinned. "I think so."

"Let's go to the corner and get a cab."

"They gonna let me into that motel, like this . . . ?" Dennis asked, tentatively, picking up the roll again. Clearly he meant the dirt.

"Don't worry," I said. "The place rents to a lot of truck drivers and working guys coming into the city. You're a working stiff who just got off work and you're going upstairs to take a shower."

"Oh . . ." Dennis said, without too much conviction.

I didn't blame him. But I knew it would pass.

At the corner, I hailed a cab, loaded Dennis into the back seat, and slid in beside him. Ten minutes later, we walked into the spiffy, be-palmed and mirrored lobby of the Skyline, Dennis in his dirt-stiff jumpsuit, no-colored wool hat, and scroungy back-pack, with his blackened face and hands. Nobody stopped us.

Up in our beige, Best Western double room, Dennis dropped his pack and immediately began to take off his clothes. "I wanna get into that shower, man," he said, getting out of his perfectly foul, padded jump suit. "I gotta take my shoes off, man," he grunted, reaching down from the edge of the bed. "I hope you got a strong stomach."

The high laced workboots, and the three layers of socks beneath them, came off—and out of them came a stench that, frankly, beats anything I've *ever* smelled before. I've put a good dozen homeless guys through their first shower in three months, in six months, in a year. But this was something else.

"When is the last time you had them off, Dennis?" I asked.

"I donno." He shrugged. "Two months. Three months, I guess." From which I assume he'd been wearing them, night and day, since mid-October. As I said, it was the end of February. The inner pair of socks had simply decayed around his feet.

Dennis went into shower — but ended up bathing, first.

Again, I've seen people take baths where the water turned gray from the dirt. But five minutes after he went in, I looked in to see how he was doing. He might as well have been sitting in a tub of India ink. Gray suds floated around the clutch of his bone-white ribs. Black trickles from his hair's wet ends tunneled down his back. If you'd poured another bottle of ink over his shoulders, what ran from his grayish hair couldn't have been blacker.

He went through a second tub of water and a second soaping. *Then* he took a shower.

Out in the room once more, toweling himself off, he said, "I guess I must be pretty clean now." His big hands were still gray, as he turned them over to examine them. But it was as though the dirt, at least there, had become part of him.

Next we sat down on the bed, and began to talk.

Then we lay down.

And held each other. For about two days.

A couple of interchanges from it all:

"How come I told you so much about me?" Dennis asked me, once. "I don't understand that. I don't know you. Yet, I can't seem to stop talking about myself. I ain't told nobody this much about me in my whole life — I didn't even know there was this much about me to tell!"

Once, in the middle of the night, he got sick — and threw up in the John toilet. I held his head, cleaned him up, put him back to bed, and rubbed his back till he fell asleep. (It wasn't drink; we'd had no more than two beers apiece, but whatever had given him the shits earlier that night must have caught up to him.) Later he was feeling a little better, and we had more sex.

At another point (day or night, I'm not sure), we lay holding each other in the dark room and watched, silently, almost in awe, a PBS TV show on the formation of the universe, with spiraling, flaring images of the forming planets, comets, and stars.

At still another, squatting naked in the middle of the floor, beside the pile of discarded clothing (we'd agreed he had to throw at least half of it away, as is was too filthy and/or rotten through to salvage), Dennis unpacked and repacked his whole backpack: two rolls of toilet paper, some clean clothes he'd forgotten someone had given him several months ago, a cassette radio/recorder, some tape cassettes (Ray Stevens, Carly Simon, Crystal Gayle, Charlie Daniels, Moms Mabley, Pete Fountain . . .) some cooking pots, some silverware, a box of sugar, bunches of papers, endless folded up plastic bags . . .

He arranged all of it, meticulously across the motel carpet, each item square with each other item, then, still naked, his grayish hair around his shoulders (although he is not, by any one's notion, a muscular man, there's no fat on him at all), he repacked it.

On his tape player, Dennis played me a cassette of Andrew Dice Clay, and we laughed at its absurd vulgarity.

His comment on the time we were together (which, yes, included pretty constant sex) was: "I guess we do get along pretty well."

A couple of times I suggested that Dennis leave the hotel (with me) to get food. But he didn't want to. So I went out (in the pouring rain, at three in the morning) to bring back sandwiches and sodas from the all-night deli across 10th Avenue, pondering as I crossed the splattering asphalt, that we were only a block or so away from where, sixty years before, Balanchine had set his "Slaughter on 10th Avenue . . ." ballet, whose music I'd so loved as a kid. I also brought back an aerosol can of room deodorizer. Even with Dennis showered and dried, the smell in the room from the clothing was pretty fierce to walk in on. On the second day, we began to talk about the possibility of my taking him up to Amherst. He'd like that, he said.

Then, toward the end of the second day, something strange happened — at least, it was strange to me.

We were sleeping. I wasn't quite sure whether it was day or night. Dennis moved away from me, got up, went to the bathroom to take a leak, came out and, from the middle of the floor said, "I think I'm gonna go, now."

Rolling over, I blinked in the half dark, with light just from the bathroom, and said: "Okay."

Over the next twenty-five minutes, he got himself back into his several layers of clothing (leaving aside the ones we'd agreed he'd better just throw away). He repacked his backpack.

I made no protests.

Once I suggested that he keep the key, since the room way paid for over another night. "You can always come back here, wash up if you want — maybe get some more sleep. I won't bother you."

"Naw," he said. "That's all right."

I went out with him. It was still raining.

"I'm going to take a cab home," I told him. "You want me to drop you off at 72nd Street?"

"Yeah," he said.

So I hailed a taxi and we got in. After a moment, he said: "You can let me off a couple of blocks before 72nd Street. That'd be better."

"Sure," I said, still without questioning. At 68th street, I told the cab driver to pull up. There was a rather fancy Chinese restaurant there, with a red and gold awning. Later I wrote in my journal

(Jan 21st, 1990):

. . . Dropped him, with knapsack and sleeping roll off, in a cab, at 69th and 10th — he wanted to be let out a few blocks before 72nd. The rain

began to pound like hail as he slid out, dragging his gear. I saw him, in his long hair and gray woolen hat, hurry over to a doorway. And rode home through the wet morning.

(I note that before and aft of this entry are attempts at a poem based on Hölderlin's "Bread and Wine," and some comments on the Paul de Man essay on the same poem.)

I figured that was probably the end of it. I'd see Dennis again, I figured; and we'd probably still be friends. But I was certain that was the end of anything physical between us. I had no idea what had occurred inside him. The sex had seemed satisfying enough, both to him and to me. I wondered what it would have been like to have had him up at Amherst.

When I'd first come to the hotel room, I'd brought three six-packs of beer. But we hadn't even killed one of them. So, back at my apartment, discussing all this with John Del Gaizo, I asked him to come down and pick up the remaining half case and we'd take it home. I'd told him about Dennis's foot stench. But when we walked into the room, though by now it had been made up and I'd long since thrown out the offending socks in the garbage can out on the corner and sprayed the room well (several times over) with deodorizer and left the windows wide — and though Dennis and every trace of his gear had been gone from the room a good six hours by then —, John, when he stepped into the room, threw out his hands, reeled back against the door. "Jesus!" he exclaimed. "What died in here?"

"That's Dennis's feet," I told him.

I'm really surprised they didn't charge me something extra, or at least say something to me at the desk when I checked out. But they didn't. They were going to find that room unrentable for the next couple of days.

I must have gone back up to Amherst a few days later. Though it has nothing directly to do with Dennis, perhaps the following journal entry explains some of what happened next. Though undated, it was written, here in my Amherst apartment, less than two weeks on, when I had just assumed my position as Acting Department Head in Professor Marc Shell's absence and we'd just gone through registration:

"The sad and almost weekly reiterated truth is that I am not happy here.

"Waking in the snow-blanketed morning, and wandering across the great orange rug (my mother's) in my study, to gaze out on the snow blurred dawn, wrapped round with fog, I'm confronted with the fundamental peacefulness and serenity of the town as a physical place. But the moment the fog burns off, I'm confronted with its equally fundamental impoverishments — financial, cultural, and social.

"On Monday, registration day, I got into the office about seven-thirty. The line from the Comp. Lit. door wound down, out the building, down the ramp, and on for another seventy-five feet.

"As I stepped over the kids in their jeans, blue, gray, and green sweaters, some of them asleep on the hall's maroon linoleum, I asked: 'How long have you been here?'

"'Since five in the morning,' one kid told me, where he lounged with his head on a rolled sleeping bag.

"Inside, Linda — the department secretary — had just arrived, in a silvery blouse, a dark skirt, and looking perfectly green" . . .

The only point to be made further, I suppose, is that (not recorded in the entry) by the end of registration day, after sitting at and working on the registration desk (more than one graduate student, passing by in the confusion of slightly frantic undergraduates, commented that they'd never seen the chairman even in the office on registration day, much less working the desk; but I wanted to see how the process functioned), I realized that we should have had at least another two hundred places for students in our Gen Ed. classes; but, part of the political game we are all playing with the Provost is that, if they wont/can't give us the money, we won't teach the students.

Though one was painfully aware that we could have. But this had all been set up before I had anything to do with it.

Really, it was very depressing, though, turning kid after kid away because there were no more places open.

In the midst of all this, Del Gaizo phoned me up with some extraordinarily good advice. "Chip," he said. "You're going to have to have a talk with Iva."

"Mmmm," I said. "About what?"

"Your sex life."

"How do you mean?" I asked, though I pretty much knew.

"She's sixteen — and you have one."

Two weeks later, I was back down in New York. On a bright, cold, morning, around eleven, I decided to walk past Dennis's spot and say hello if he was there. It never occurred to me that we would have any more to do with each other sexually. But I just wanted to reestablish friendly relations. At that hour, the block is very busy with people marching along all over the place, so you can't see very far along it.

But Dennis must have caught sight of me the same time I saw him. He came running up to me, grinning. "Hey, yeah!" was the first thing he said.

"Huh?"

"Yeah, I wanna go up there with you — to Boston!" Dennis had never quite gotten straight that I was teaching in Amherst, not Boston.

"It's Amherst, Dennis," I said.

"Well, wherever. I wanna get out of this fuckin' city, man! We get along, real good, too. An' I really wanna go!"

"Well," I said. "I've got a conference to go to out in California at the end of this week. So I wouldn't be able to take you for — well, say, two weeks."

"That's okay," he said. "I been out here for fuckin' six years. I can wait two weeks more."

"How come you got up and just left like that?"

"I don't know," he said pensively. "I just wanted to get out and think it over. And you didn't try and stop me or anything. That was good. So I thought about it. An' I wanna go, now."

I thought for a moment. Then I grinned back. "Okay. Two weeks from now, when I come in, we'll go on up there."

Later that day, when Iva came over, I did have a talk with her. It occurs to me that this talk is a lot harder — and more necessary — than the rather mechanical "birds & bees" discussion one has with a ten/eleven/twelve year old.

Iva sat on the living room couch. I sat in the corner by the bookshelf. "You know," I began, and of course found myself hoping that, at sixteen, she knew much more than she probably could. "Well . . . you know, your dad is a pretty full functioning adult. And, for better or for worse, I have a sex life."

"Oh, I know," she said.

"Well, I don't know how much you know. So I have to talk to you about some of this. The idea isn't to embarrass you. But I have to talk to you because I don't want you to be embarrassed, or confused, or upset about things that might happen later on. You've had a boyfriend, now. You'll probably have another one soon. You have your own interest in sex . . ." Realizing of course, I had no idea how to go on with this. "Look, I don't have anyone I'm steadily seeing now. But I'd like to. And someday I'd like to live with somebody again, the way I used to live with Frank. If I do, I want you to know that it doesn't mean I love you any the less. Or that I'm going to forget about you in any way. But it's something that would be nice. And if it happens, I want you to understand it."

"Oh, I will," she said.

"Good." Other than in some very passing fantasy, I don't think I really considered that that person might be Dennis. I figured, rather, he'd come up for a couple of weeks, then go back to the city. And maybe we'd do it again some other time, after another few months or a year.

About a week later, however, I called John Del Gaizo from Amherst. Would he go down, give Dennis ten bucks for me, and also hang out with him for a while, talk to him, have coffee with him or a beer, and then tell me what his opinion of Dennis was. There was something about this that was very crazy. But there was something else that seemed eminently sane.

The night before I was supposed to come down to the city, John phoned me up, while I sat at my back room desk, with the spring halogen light on now, John explained: "Well, last evening, after work, I spent about an hour standing on the street and having coffee with Dennis. He's a very gentle man."

"Yeah," I said. "He is."

"And he likes you a lot." Then he asked. "Does he know you're a writer?"

"No," I said. "I don't think I ever told him. He knows I teach."

"*Mmm*," John said. "That's what I gathered."

"Do you think I'm totally out of my mind?"

"Well," John said. "You say he's not into drugs. He doesn't steal. And he does what he says he's going to do"—these were all things I'd pretty much established about Dennis over the months since I'd first started talking to him—"I'd say he was about perfect for you. Try it."

The next day, I took the five o'clock in the morning Peter Pan bus down from Amherst. At Port Authority in New York, I bought two round trip bus tickets, and took a cab up to 72nd Street.

Dennis was there, standing in his usual spot, and I showed him the tickets. "Yeah," he said, thoughtfully. "You don't bullshit people. I knew that, when you came here and showed me the hotel room keys. Lot of people, they're always tellin' you what they're gonna do for you—then you never see them again. But you ain't like that. So we goin' up there?"

"On Monday," I said. "You want to stay out here and watch your cars today? I'll pick you up tonight. You can sleep at my place tonight. And on Monday, we'll take a bus up to Amherst, early in the morning."

"Okay," he said. "Good."

And that's what we did. The first night he stayed at my place, he was sick again—but I think you just pick up a load of minor viruses, living rough like that. Over the next days, I brought him some clothes. We left the knapsack behind in my New York office and the jumpsuit for John to take to the cleaners.

Dennis came up here in the first week in March—he's been here since. And, basically, I'm as happy as a pig in shit!

One thing I told him, when he got here: "Dennis, I like you a lot. So try to make up your mind about whether you want to stay here within the first six weeks. If you decide you don't like it and you want to go back, it'll be pretty easy on me. But if you decide to go after six or seven months, that's going to be kind of hard. Okay?"

"Okay," he said.

Around the first six weeks, I asked him how the whole thing seemed to him. There were lots of things—like showering—he had to do. He'd had to get his hair cut—his first in six years. He got his second a few days ago, and now looks rather like a marine lifer. He's met people, and, always an affable guy, he's been pretty sociable. All in all, I asked him, when we got half way through the second month, was this better than being out on the street?

He mused: "I never ate so many strange foods before in my life. I never ate no mushrooms before. I never ate no strawberries." (At one local restaurant here, he's discovered fresh strawberry shortcake.) "I never had no Chinese food. I didn't even know what blueberry pancakes was." This is now his standard breakfast at the breakfast place down the street. "I didn't even know you had two kinds of syrup." (For 95 cents extra you can get real maple syrup.) "Is this better than being on the street? Are you fuckin' *crazy*?"

So we laughed. And are still "getting along real well." Neither one of us has had occasion to raise his voice to the other in the three months he'd been here — much less have an argument.

I also learned that, while he was considering coming, Dennis was also busily "checking you out, man. 'Cause you coulda been psycho, you know. You could have got me up here and cut me up in little pieces and buried 'em all over the place — an' nobody'd ever knowed shit about it."

Back in the city, he'd asked a gay cop friend (Officer Nick Antonelli) what he thought of the whole business; Antonelli, whom I've since met, told him, sensibly enough: "Dennis, if he was going to do any weird sexual stuff to you, he'd've done that back in the motel room. So if that part worked out well, and you like him, I'd try it out."

The most extraordinary of coincidences, however, was this.

One of Dennis's many New York friends, who's given him a hand or helped him out over the years, is a guy named Jim Yurgan. Jim is another middle class black guy, a year younger than I am, who used to go to Dalton back when I did. Jim was also a member of the Jack and Jill Club with me, and he's now married and a film maker. Apparently Jim used to bring Dennis food regularly. So when Dennis saw him on the street, he told Jim there was this guy who'd offered to take him up to Massachusetts and let him stay there with him. ("Now I didn't tell anybody — except Nick, 'cause he's gay too — about the sex. I figure that's just between you and me. But I told him you was gonna take me up there, give me a hand, help me get back on my feet. I figured, probably, some of 'em would figure out about the sex, and the ones who couldn't, it wasn't none of their business, anyway.") What did Jim think about that?

"What's his name?" Jim had asked.

"Chip Delany," Dennis had told him. "He's some kind of Professor."

"No kidding," Jim had said. "Is he a black guy?"

"About as black as you are," Dennis said.

"Yeah, I know him. I used to go to school with him. Today, he's a very well known science fiction writer."

So, apparently, Dennis *had* known something about my reputation by the time he agreed to come up here after all!

"But when Jim said he'd been in school with you, I figured you couldn't be too crazy. An' he said I should try it out, too. So I decided if you was a friend of Jim's, you couldn't be but so bad—'cause he been helpin' me out on the street almost two years now."

Small world.

One slight marring to an otherwise perfect friendship: two weeks later, Dennis and I came down to New York for a long weekend. In the course of things, I had to buy some underwear for both Dennis and me. I'd gone down to Robbin's, on 38th Street and Eighth Avenue. It was raining. I had one of those small, black, Taiwanese umbrellas. My glasses were somewhat splattered, and, with underwear bundled under one arm, with half a dozen other people I was about to cross from the South West to the South East corner of the street at Eighth and 42nd, to catch the 104 bus—

The next thing I knew, I was lying on the pavement. My umbrella was blowing away from me over the wet sidewalk. But I couldn't see it very clearly, because my glasses were gone.

Apparently, coming around the corner, the van of a truck had side-swiped me, spun me around, and knocked me four feet across the sidewalk. The blow and the fall, I simply don't remember—although there's a vague recollection of something large and grey coming by me at about that time. I may well have lost consciousness for a second or two.

About fifteen people gathered around to help me up. One young lady in a white sweater ran out into the street to retrieve my glasses—mercifully unbroken.

Then we began what turned into two days of trying to report it to the police. (Right after it happened, in pain and the pouring rain, I went to three different places—at the instruction of various policemen—none of which were able to take the report!) But the long and short of it is, however, that I busted a rib low on my left side. Two and a half months later, it's still pretty painful in some positions. But—praise the lord—though it occasionally wakes me up at night (and only about a month ago I had to make an emergency trip into Cooley Dickinson Hospital, over in Northampton, because after a day spent more or less in one position reading, it grew so painful I could hardly bear it), it doesn't interfere with sex.

At the third week of April, we came down to New York again for a week, and I went to the Ring at the Met—this time with Professor Don Levine, who also teaches here at U. Mass. It was a wondrously warm week. For most of the four evenings, we'd meet, have dinner (twice with Dennis, once with Barbara Wise, and once with just the two of us) at Marvin Gardens on Broadway or the Empire Grill across from Lincoln Center, then we'd go down and take in the next opera.

On the evening of *Siegfried*, Don and I were sitting at the outside tables on the avenue, when who wandered by but bushy-haired composer, Anthony (*X, The Life and Times of Malcolm X*) Davis. He stopped to say hello, to introduce us to the zaftig soprano tucked under his arm (and with whom, apparently, he is now living), and said: "By the way, Chip—would you like to write an opera with me?"

"I'd love to," I said.

"Good," he said. "Let's do it."

Then, after an exchange of addresses, he walked on. So I think, if his interest remains, I shall.

This season's *Götterdämmerung* was memorable for its last minutes, in which, when Hildegard Behrens (not in the best of voice for the cycle, since she had a cold throughout) turned to run to the back of the stage and throw herself on Siegfried's flaming pyre, the Hall of the Gibichungs, which collapses so spectacularly in this production (I saw it last season, too, with Gwyneth Jones), began to collapse about seven seconds early—the first great beam that fell hit her on the head and knocked her sprawling—

A dozen supers and chorus members ran over to her, as the set began to sink into the stage, and the rest of the collapse took place around her. But she never made it to the funeral pyre. A couple of other cues in the closing moments were off too—the Rhine, as far as I could tell, never did flood properly (as it had in last year's production, if my memory is right), though the bottom of the river rose up and Hagen leapt in and was drowned by the Rhinemaidens, while he called out the opera's closing words, "*Zurück vom Ring!*"

In the distance, Valhalla flamed briefly and vanished. The populace was left, among the fallen castle's stone, staring out over the waters, as we heard the "Praise Brunnhilde" motif close out the opera, resolving on its terminal D-flat major chord.

But the accident had looked so traumatic, that by this point half the audience was standing and buzzing.

After the curtain fell, the stage manager came out and made an announcement that Behrens was, indeed, all right—but that there would be no curtain calls that night.

Don and I left the Met, a-buzz with the rest of the audience, for the Broadway hamburger joint a few blocks north where, each night, we'd gone to dissect the performance and drift into general gossip.

Just as we were crossing mid-night Broadway, there was a three-car accident across the Avenue from us (smash! *Bang!* Screech! Crash!), and, through the neon streamed windows of the restaurant, we watched the ambulances and police cars for the next forty minutes.

Back in Amherst, my last days of classes were rather strange.

As Acting Head of my department this term, I taught only a single seminar ("Prospero, Leonardo, Freud"), with only nine students—four of whom were graduates and five of whom were undergraduates. Paradoxically, I was far more pleased in general with the work the undergraduates did than I was with the graduates. My most articulate woman graduate was a young woman named Jamee Saliba—who alas had a bad case of "canonitis." She couldn't figure out any reason to read anything that wasn't on the list of great approved works that she'd heard of many times before. And we were reading Auden's "The Sea and the Mirror" and Aimé Césaire's "Une Tempête" and his "Discours sur le colonialisme" and Freud and Shakespeare and Merezhkovsky's "Christ and Antichrist" trilogy, and Vasari and Pater and Valéry . . .

A week before the end of the class, she asked to withdraw. This is highly irregular, and I should have said no (so all my colleagues informed me). Her reason was "lack of interest in the material," most of which she had not been able to bring herself to read, anyway. But as an extremely articulate woman, her complaints had really done more to hold back than to help the class and I was simply happy to have her gone. Only after she left did I learn she was only twenty-two — only a year older than one of my undergraduates. I'd just assumed she was thirty or older. I don't know whether I would have handled her any differently or not had I known.

Still, it left a rather odd taste with me — if you know what I mean.

The discovery of the year was a young man from Hampshire College, named David Claussen, who is only a 19-year-old sophomore, but who is clearly brilliant and doubtless harbors great things within him. He's skinny, has long curly black hair, wears glasses — he was fascinated by everything we looked at and wrote wonderful, excited, passionate papers about it all.

A few weeks after the Ring proper, after going through the Francis Bacon retrospective, in the restaurant at the Museum of Modern Art, Barbara Wise and I were musing over glasses of white wine, when she suggested that she get tickets for Iva and me for the final performance of the Ridiculous Theatrical Company's spoof, *Der Ring Gott Farblonjet*. "After all," she said, "Iva saw the real thing with you last year. And you've seen the real thing twice." [Three times, actually, but who's counting.] "You must be ready to giggle at it a bit by now."

And so we did.

Barbara's dear friend Harry Katoukas was in the cast, playing "Eartha, the Earth Mutter." And for the farewell performance, Barbara had ordered a cake for the cast party in the theater right afterwards. (I went across Sixth Avenue and picked up the cake — seventy-nine dollars worth.) The only hitch was that Barbara had thought the curtain was at eight, when it was actually at seven-thirty. So we arrived (the staff in the theater still a-hum, because James Levine [the conductor at the Met] had shown up that evening in the audience) a bit after things had started.

Barbara had seen it before, so she insisted I go in. Then she went out to wait for Iva, and ten minutes later I saw them come through the hanging over the door.

We more or less missed all-but-the-tail-end of *Rhinegold*. But the rest was truly clever, funny, and obviously done by someone who knew and loved the Ring well—and it beats out even Anna Russell for belly laughs.

Afterwards, the considerable cast hung around the theater for beer, cold cuts, wine, and more goodies—climaxed by Barbara's sumptuous cake.

I had a good time. Iva had a good time.

And Barbara, who was just a bit miffed over having gotten the wrong time, finally calmed down and decided to enjoy herself too. It was really a wonderful evening.

An interesting phenomenon, back at Amherst, on the next to last day when I had any real Chair-work to do. (Is that like char-work? *Mmmm . . .*) I'd come into the office, and I was writing a pro forma recommendation for a soon to be retiring professor, whom we had managed to get out of our department last term and shunt him over into English, where he belongs. I'd worked with the man on the Personnel Committee—and frankly I think he's certifiably nuts. He managed to reach retirement without ever having published a book. His only claim to fame is that he has memorized the first few fyts of Beowulf, which he goes around reciting to anyone who will listen.

They want him to give a Distinguished Faculty Lecture before he goes (for which, I suspect, he will recite an hour of Beowulf in Olde English, since that's all he can do) so that he can be sent off with honor and dignity. And the recommendation I'd been asked to write was to enable him to give said lecture.

As I was sitting there, halfway through this meaningless piece of verbiage (". . . his high intellectual standards and admirable service on the Personnel Committee were appreciated by the whole department . . ."), I found myself typing out . . . the truth: ". . . When he served on the Personnel Committee, his faulty arithmetic repeatedly resulted in figures which said that he was to receive two and a half times more merit money than anyone else in the department. When this was pointed out to him—twice—both times he offered a flustered apology. But, on a third try, with the help of a calculator, he seemed unable to divide by twelve and get the proper figure—this time it came out that he was to receive *four* times as much money as anyone else—he was relieved of the job, and the Associate Chair, in two minutes, produced figures that the rest of the committee found acceptable." And I began to laugh.

And was unable to stop.

A few minutes later, the phone rang, and I picked it up—to a request that I prepare some statement on the accomplishments of the Comparative Literature Cross Cultural Committee for that term: the Cross Cultural Committee had met three times, and had hired an African graduate student for secretarial work who had only shown up in the office once, though he continued to collect a weekly salary. When I was finally called in on this (by the irate and distraught committee), I called said young man, who offered to return the money, since, by his own admission, he'd done nothing for it; but our secretary informed us we had no way of accepting the money back in the department so that it would work out on the books. And the former chairman, when I called him for advice, raised his eyes to heaven, sighed, and said that, this late in the term, we'd best let him go on collecting till the end of the term and just swallow the loss—hoping that we not do anything quite so stupid next term.

I began to laugh again.

At this point, I excused myself from the gentleman on the phone. Then I went into the reception area, and told Linda (our department secretary): "Linda," I said. "I've got to go home. I've just had an attack of the sillies. And it's perfectly clear that I'm not going to get any more work done this morning, if I stay here."

She smiled and said, "Yes, Chip—there are days I understand that sort of thing around here all too well."

So I went home.

By the next morning, I was pretty much recovered. In the office by eight, I finished the recommendation as well as two or three other pieces of busy work—without cracking a giggle.

But about quarter to ten, I decided to nip over to the student union to pick up a container of coffee—as the office pot ceases to function once final exams are over with.

As I was going down the wheelchair-accessible ramp to the building (built three years ago at a cost of five thousand dollars, it [one] means everyone else entering the building must now walk about twenty yards out of the way, and [two] it decants the prospective wheelchair roller into a hall before a set of marble steps in a building sans elevator: our wheelchair-bound philosophy graduate student, Andy Blaze, who does not come to see me in my office on the third floor, says it's a joke in very bad taste), I saw a bunch of Freshmen students milling about beside the rhododendrons. They all happened to be young women. Most were in various beige or brown or yellow Bermudas. They weren't chewing gum, but I was aware that fifteen years ago most of them would have been.

About a third of them had the bemused expression of people who are just beginning to realize that the person they are waiting for probably is wholly unaware that they are waiting — and, in any case, he or she is not going to show up. Four or five of them had fallen into cheerful gossip to pass away the time. And as I passed, listening to one explain to two others, ". . . he was so angry; I mean, he was just so angry — Genie was just sitting there . . . and I didn't know what to do; I just thought it was so funny. But he was just furious . . . !" it hit me:

These kids aren't going to learn *anything* at this school. Pretty much everything they are going to know intellectually they already knew by age twelve. The personalities will change, even mature, and strengthen. But no learning will take place here that's worth the name. It *can't* at this school.

I began to laugh again.

And there went the rest of the day — though, somehow, I managed to get through it in the office. And by the time I strolled home, I'd actually gotten *through the last list* of things to do before handing the Chairmanship back to Professor Shell — who officially resumes it on July 1st.

Shortly after that, I picked up a copy of the *New York Times Book Review* at Albion Books, here in town, and, while reading a review by Irving Howe of a book about a young, dedicated teacher, working in a school for underprivileged children, found myself deeply moved.

Ah, yes — another tale of Dennis. (Our closest thing to an adventure, since he's been staying with me.) But I will simply relate the first part of it out of my journal:

May 25th: Today an irate and upset Dennis loped into my office while I was typing my letter to Professor McCracken. "Do you know what happened to me!" he demanded, seeming much larger than his usual five-foot ten.

"What?" I turned from the graphite colored screen, a-scatter with white letters.

He leaned down and, from under his red baseball cap, stared into my face, wide eyed: "I got *arrested*!" Then his head swung away, as he paced (in one and a half steps) back to the door. I thought he was about to leave — only then he was back, bending over me: "For exposing myself!"

"Huh?"

And as he drew away, with the uncharacteristic pacer's agitation: "I got arrested for exposing myself!": He was wearing his very soiled grey sweat pants, with a couple of black grease smears across the thighs, his old running shoes that I'd gotten for Bobby [a homeless man with serious short term memory impairment] some months before, but had never been able to find him again to give them to him and a quilted black jacket over his equally soiled sweat shirt. "Chip, I'm gettin' out of this fuckin' town! I come here to get away from shit like that! For God damn exposing myself. Can you believe that? I'm sorry, I'm leaving here—"

"Dennis, what happened?" Looking at him, in the sweatsuit clinging to his gaunt, wiry frame, I couldn't help recalling *that*, one, he's hung like the proverbial mule, and, two, in such informal attire, it shows.

"I was down behind the graveyard, with my bike, drinking some water — when they came up to me and took me in."

"Where?"

"To the police station. They took me to the police station. They took my picture!"

"Did they fingerprint you?"

"No. But they took my picture." He shook his head, reaching behind him for the door knob. "I've had it with this town. I'm leavin'," and, behind the swinging panel of gray, he was out in the hall.

I was up to follow him. But he was already out the door at the hall's head.

I went out and looked down over the banister and the margin of the marble steps. "Dennis . . ."

Footsteps were hammering down.

"Dennis, come on back here now and talk to me . . . Dennis?"

But the steps did not reverse.

I went back through the door, into the hall, and into my office.

I sat down at the word processor again.

I certainly didn't think he'd done it. Dennis had been over his minuscule perversions with me—other than enjoying two-man/one-woman threesomes, there really weren't any—and flashing just wasn't among them.

I figured the best thing for him would to ride around and work it off for a while (clearly he'd come here to my office on his bike); if he didn't turn up at home and one of the return trip tickets was gone when I got back, I'd phone John Del Gaizo in New York, and tell him to be on the lookout for our wandering boy. (Was this, I wondered, going to be the end of our two months of so far very pleasant living together?) I looked over my letter to Professor McCracken, and didn't see very much of it. And the information I needed from Linda to complete it wasn't available anyway, since she was out of the office for another hour . . .

About eight minutes later, the door pushed open again, and Dennis stepped inside.

"Come in," I said, swiveling away from the Zenith screen, "sit down, now, and tell me everything that happened."

The greater story, which was still gaining details a day later, seems to be this:

Dennis was out riding his bike, had stopped behind the graveyard (where Ms. Dickinson lies buried) near the Pray Street entrance, to take a drink of water from the "Budweiser" plastic bike water bottle clipped to his frame, when a middle-aged policemen got out of a car and asked him for some identification. Dennis didn't have any, of course. And the policemen—very politely, Dennis said—asked him to come to the police station. Dennis, equally politely, asked what for? The policemen explained that someone had reported that somebody was running around exposing himself. A bit flustered and surprised, Dennis began to explain that he was staying with Professor Delany, Professor Delany had been giving him a hand after he had spent six years as a homeless person, living on the street, but he hadn't done anything wrong. The policemen let Dennis ride his bike and follow the car to the station. After that, they let him go.

It sounded strange to me, so I called the police station. Dennis was still pretty upset. I got a woman police clerk who told me that, indeed,

there had been half a dozen reports of a flasher in the neighborhood
—it had been in the local papers for several days now. He'd been described as white, wore gym pants and a baseball cap (which narrows it
to perhaps twenty percent of the male student population of U. Mass!),
and the police were simply pulling in people for questioning who fit
that description.

I told her how upset my friend was. She said please, he mustn't take it
personally. And if they had let him go, then there certainly was no more
suspicion. I relayed this to Dennis, and over the next forty-eight hours
he pretty much calmed down about it. Soon it was just a joke to bring
out with the waitresses in the Café, where we breakfast, and in Charlie's,
the townie bar where Dennis goes for beer.

Two months later, it's all-but forgotten, except to laugh over. But it
was quite an adventure, while it was happening.

We came back to New York for a while only a day or two later, which
probably helped in the cooling off period. But on my first day in the
city, I had an interesting revelation about my "attack of the sillies," that
I wrote you about above.

I'd taken the bus across Central Park to visit Books & Co., on Madison
Avenue. It's right next to the Whitney Museum, so, since I was there, I
decided to go on in.

It was Wednesday, I believe, when the museum has various groups
of school children in. The student groups were largely black and Hispanic, and the guides, mostly young white female art students, were
going around with them, from gallery to gallery, telling them about the
paintings and the painters. I followed one group, and was incredibly
impressed with the job the guide was doing. She would go right to the
most visible aspect of the painting, that all the kids could see, and then
move on to more subtle things—and she was keeping the kids absolutely fascinated and had their total attention.[8] And what she was telling

---

8. I have told and written about this incident many times since: The particular
painting was a Willem de Kooning canvas from his series "Women," and had
oversized, swirling breasts, and the question to the young black and Hispanic
public school visitors was: What's the most obvious thing you can see about this
painting, and the answer—with giggles, after an embarrassed moment—was

them were the kinds of things that, indeed, make art the wonderful and rich experience that it is. After five minutes, I found myself in silent tears —following a little bit behind, not making a sound, but with the tears simply cascading from my eyes, while I tried to wipe them away.

The young woman was someone who clearly had spent lots of time figuring out the way to get through to these children—and the way to present this material so that it was comprehensible and rich for them. What I was crying for was simply that here, real learning was occurring. Underneath the "sillies" up at Amherst there'd been a whole lot of very real frustration.

I'm not a bad teacher. At the end of my "Introduction to Science Fiction" class, last term, my whole hall of a hundred students gave me a solid round of applause.

But neither am I an unswervingly great one. And I haven't figured out an entire battery of techniques to break through to my white, working class, well-brought up, but hugely intellectually underprivileged students. Nor, really, is that what I want to do with my life. But the fact that the guide at the Whitney had taken up her job so well with these socially deprived kids from Brooklyn simply made me cry—with a kind of joy and relief that, indeed, someone had been able to assume their heuristic responsibilities better than, in the long run, I have been able to.

A final snap shot.

In New York, Dennis and Iva and John and I were all sitting around the living room. Nobody was paying particular attention to the TV— which was showing a PBS documentary on penguins. But, now Dennis, now John, now Iva, and at last me, began to watch it.

After a half an hour, when the program ended, Dennis, sitting cross-legged on the rug, turned to me, where I sat in the corner chair, and said,

---

"Her breasts . . . !" or "Her titties . . ." to which the guide responded enthusiastically, "YES!" and went on to talk about their size, their colors, the importance of breasts in the human body, and how all these things were figured in painting itself. The further point is that the young museum guide was acting far more of a sexual radical than I was in my all too discreet 1989 epistolary account of what she had done, though I certainly responded emotionally to its force and intelligence, in terms of utilizing the social forces to strengthen her pedagogical success. (SRD, 2017) softly, but with a hint of an ironic smile: "That was almost as profound as the creation of the universe, I guess."

Anyway, I must wind this up, as we've got a bus to catch back to the city in twenty-five minutes.

Love and stuff,
to you and Cynthia
and the boys and
the little creatures too —

Samuel R. Delany

3

TO ROBERT BRAVARD

January 28, 1991

• • •

21 Cowles Lane

Amherst, MA 01002

January 28th, 1991

Dear Bob,

I'm starting this in my office, about 7:50 am, on Monday morning —registration day.[9] The building is stifling hot—as, earlier, a rain has brought the outside temperature of the snow-scabbed countryside up into the high thirties or low forties, while the building thermostat is still set for the three and four degrees we've been having here in Amherst for the past week. The hall outside my office is stuffed with pleasant, sleepy kids in sweatshirts, sweaters, baseball caps, and sweat pants, waiting for us to start registering them for classes. Many have been here since five o'clock this morning. Three or four are curled on the hall carpet asleep. When I got in, about twenty minutes ago, I opened two of the windows in the reception area, which should bring the temperature down a bit nearer the bearable. A couple of the kids looked thankfully at me as I pried loose the all-but-stuck white window frames.

Winding through the crush back to my office seemed a bit much, so I just sat down and read till our department secretary, Linda, got in— about ten minutes ago.

She's making coffee, now.

We officially start at eight-thirty.

Let me see if I can bring you up to date.

After a one-term research (read: writing) leave, I'm again Acting Head of our Department.

During my three months off, I completed a long short story, "*Citre*

---

9. Spring registration a year after the previous letter. (SRD)

et Trans," currently making the rounds. Some forty-five pages, it's not SF at all. Indeed, it goes back to my six months in Greece in '65/'66. I'm very pleased with it. But so far it's been rejected by both *Antaeus* and *Grand Street*—though with encouraging letters from both Halpern and Jean Stein. Currently it's out on the coast at *Fiction International*, where, frankly, I think it's got the best chance.

In the last three months I've completed (and published) three long-ish articles for the *New York Review of Science Fiction*, the last of which was a review of Antonia Susan Byatt's *Possession*, which, basically, I enjoyed. Byatt, incidentally, is Margaret Drabble's sister.

I'll send you on a copy of my remarks, since you mention it—favorably—in your last letter.

I also got through another "K. L. Steiner" article, which may or may not appear in a special issue of the *Review of Contemporary Fiction* which is being edited by James Sallis and (half of which) is being devoted to my work, sometime next year.

Since the beginning of the summer, however, most of my energy has gone into what began as a long article. It surveys the work of historian-of-science and culture critic Donna Haraway. But now, however, it seems to have grown into the first four and a half chapters (more than eighty pages in pretty much finished form) of what currently I conceive as a seven chapter book/monograph on Haraway—perhaps on the order of *Wagner/Artaud*.

The working title is *Twilight in the Rue Morgue*.

I've also finished the opening fifty pages of a novel I've been contemplating for some while (years, actually), *The Dump*—as well there are notes and some firm ideas for a number of short fiction pieces, SF, horror, and other.

Reading over the list, it seems like a fairly productive three months. I, of course, experienced the time as *total* indolence, waste, and distraction from real work, which—for most of the time—seemed out of all possible reach. But then, that's how work always strikes to me. Though, I must say, I really appreciated being a free-lancer again, even for those three fraught months—there were some major interruptions in it. From last May until four days ago, Iva stayed with me and Dennis (down in New York) for all but one two-week period in September and then another three weeks in November, though she was supposed to be staying with Marilyn the whole term. But the soap-opera coefficient got a little high—what with M's lover, Karen, during a screaming and tearful argument, locking Iva (who turned seventeen on the 14th) in her room and refusing to let her go to school one odd morning back in September, while her mother was away in Ohio.

So I took over. Currently Karen is due to go in for brain (!) surgery. Iva's dry, dry comment was: "I hope they slip." Oh, well. Did I tell you, by the bye: Marilyn for the last three months has been editor of the *Kenyon Review*.

Probably the largest new thing in the material texture of my life—of the *Annales* school sort—is that the landlord finally put new hot and cold water risers into the kitchen-line of all the apartments. Since I moved into the building in '75, if one turned on the hot water in the kitchen, it was a real toss-up whether water would or would not come out of the bathroom sink faucet. Regularly I'd be in the middle of washing the dishes when suddenly the hot water would simply stop running—so that the only thing to do was to go off and do something else for anywhere between five and twenty minutes, till, with a spurt and splatter, it would start again. Nor did it *ever* come out with any force. At least one reason I've been such an early riser all these years is because, around four or five in the morning, the water is less likely to stop running than it is at eight o'clock or nine—when the other tenants start using hot water as well; a tap going on two floors below can cause mine, on the top floor, to stop flowing altogether. This has been such a common occurrence, I doubt I've ever mentioned it in all the years I've been writing to you.

It would have been like mentioning the air.

Or perhaps rigorously describing the bathroom commode.

It was simply a totally pervasive condition.

Well, now we have regular and powerful hot water. Cooking, dishwashing, and general cleanliness have all moved up three notches in their ordinary facility.

It's quite glorious.

As a good materialist, I'm waiting to be able report to you that this has had a positive effect on my work.

Give it six months.

The holidays were interesting—and, in their way, fun. (Because the period includes Christmas, Iva's birthday on the 14th of January, and now Dennis's birthday on the 24th, the period is kind of a money pit that just eats cash!) Iva had a New Year's Eve Party this year, with helium filled balloons bobbing about the ceiling, trailing their ribbons down to the rug, and everyone trooping up to our roof together at midnight, to watch the city's sparse fireworks and be terribly responsible about refusing the champagne I'd asked the kids if anyone would like a celebratory glass of. The only sadness was that Dennis and I missed each other at the midnight moment, as he'd just gone downstairs to pursue some departing children, then came up when the rest of us had gone up to the roof, and finding—suddenly—no one in the apartment and the door wide open, got confused and went back down, while I went out in the street looking for him [with two glasses of champagne in hand], while he . . . etc., etc. Eventually it all got straightened out by about twenty-past-twelve. And by one o'clock, some sixteen sixteen-year-olds went more or less to sleep in sleeping bags all over our living room and dining room floor.

The day before New Year's Eve, my sister called me to tell me that my Uncle, late-Judge Hubert T. Delany, had died. He was eighty-nine. You may remember him from that postcard of "Heroes of the Harlem Renaissance," where he stands on Regina Andrew's[10] roof on Edgecombe Avenue, with Langston Hughes and—I think—Wallace Thurman. As I'm sure I told you, since his late fifties, my uncle has suffered from a degenerative brain disease that left him all but a vegetable. I have strong and unsettling memories of the year or so in which he was slipping, when he would come to see us, have a single drink, and suddenly appear to be completely drunk—asking me or my sister the same question again and again and again, sometimes not knowing who we were or calling us by the name of one of his children or one of our cousins, while roughly waving away any attempt to quiet him or calm him or get him to go home. "There's nothing wrong with me—nothing! Nothing! Now get your hands off me!"—while his drink sloshed and spilled over the kitchen's blue vinyl flooring.

10. An acquaintance of my parents, she was also known as Regina Anderson.

My mother, at the beginning, was convinced (and disgusted by the fact) that it was advanced alcoholism — which my father always argued with, and worried about.

Only a year or so later, when we hadn't seen him at all for months, were we told that it was something else; and that he was now too far gone to leave the house. Occasionally, in those early years, Aunt Willetta would come by — a thin, elegant, pale woman, with short dark hair. "Oh, Hubert's doing very well — very well," was what she ritually answered when questioned about his condition. "He's still very confused, of course. I'll tell you," and here she might chuckle, "sometimes he doesn't even know who I am. But this morning, for instance, he was very calm. We try to keep him comfortable. Really, sometimes he flirts with the nurse unmercifully — it's almost comic. But he's doing very well."

Then, after a year or two, we saw her much less.

Till recently, I'd assumed it was Alzheimer's, but it was something else — though the results were much the same; they were complicated, in his case, by occasional loud, violent, and obscene outbursts. Willetta never put him into a nursing home. She took care of him at their Riverside Drive apartment for nearly thirty years. We all wondered how she did it, since he was also incontinent through much of that time.

But on the day before New Year's Eve, he suffered a massive heart attack. And the next day's *New York Times* carried a large obituary, taking up a quarter of the first section's back page, with a picture of him taken when, I suspect, he was not much older than I am today.

The wake was the Wednesday evening after New Year's Day, at a funeral home on St. Nicholas Avenue up at a Hundred-Forty-First Street. Because of erratic packing the last time Dennis and I came down from Amherst, I had only brown pants, a navy blue (Pierre Cardin) sports jacket — and black running shoes. It's always been my feeling that when you think you're dressed weirdly, you don't usually look anywhere near as weird as you feel. Nevertheless, with a bit of trepidation, in brown pants and black shoes, I went up to the funeral home — and don't forget my big, bushy, white beard!

I got out of the cab, crossed the freezing sidewalk in the light, light city darkness, and entered a complex of palest green and beige — walls, carpets, ceilings — that ("I'm looking for the Delany . . ." what does one say? funeral? wake? But the thin, middle-aged black woman in the bright red blazer, from her chartreuse cubicle behind the glass, smiled and pointed me along a hall) finally emptied me, along with another gentleman about my age who'd joined me at the information window, into a large, lime colored chapel, full of relatives and friends I hadn't seen for twenty years — as well as many I'd never seen at all!

In ten minutes, a dozen faces presented themselves — to be transformed by gestalt shift into the faces of people, known years and years ago at family gatherings and only just remembered: hugs and kisses for the women, hand-shakes (often with a second hand placed warmly atop the first) for the men — and one little black-brown guy with a spade-shaped chin, no lower teeth, and a carpet of white hair suddenly threw his arms around me and hugged me hard, crying out: "Little Sam . . . !"

And, a moment later, I realized that this was someone who had been one of my father's twenty-five-year-old, devilishly handsome and high spirited employees, back when I was fifteen or sixteen (his tendency to youthful irresponsibility had always worried my father), now a fifty-eight-year-old funeral director himself.

While we enthused at one another, grinning, I was uncomfortably aware that I couldn't remember his name!

I spoke — and was physically tugged down to sit beside — my Aunt Willetta . . . by Aunt Francis, whom I hadn't seen for several years: she's not really my aunt; nevertheless I always called her that. Her husband, "Uncle" Bill, once took a lovely photograph of me and my sister when we were three and two: the little white table, covered with a white blanket where we sat, me in seersucker shorts and sandals, my sister clutching a yarn doll, under his lights, me with my arm around her shoulder, with Uncle Bill and his lamps and his tripodded camera, jockeying for the best shot, and my great happiness and positive excitement over it all, is still as vivid as any of my childhood memories. Their two daughters, Linda and Jane, eventually went to Dalton with me — Linda in my class and Jane a year ahead.

Jane, with her husband, a white man named Robert, actually lived on the same block that I do, currently; and, perhaps five years ago, one night at about nine, when I was coming home, I saw Robert, in his rain coat, striding angrily up the street, while Jane, a tall, slender woman, but then in bathrobe and slippers, ran after her husband, crying: "Oh, Robert—no . . . ! Please, Robert . . . Oh, Robert, please . . ." the two of them passing me, oblivious, and disappearing at the corner, while, curious, I turned onto my stoop to go upstairs.

But now Aunt Francis poured into my ear one of those odd and surreal stories, rendered so strange because (at least one reason) it presumes you know so much more about things than you do: ". . . Oh, Sam, it was so odd—last year, the day Robert—you know, Jane's husband —died: Uncle Bill was so sick. He died the very next day—poor Jane, she hasn't been back to the apartment since. (Now, if you see her, you mustn't tell her I told you that! But I think she's beginning to feel a little better about things—she was right down there with you, wasn't she?) She told me, just this morning, she really must get herself together and go back there and start doing some thing about all that stuff this week. I think Hubert's death made her realize you just can't avoid certain things like that. Promise me, now, that you'll give Linda a call. She was always so fond of you—and I know she'd love to hear from you . . ."

While, on the other side of me, Aunt Willetta was saying: "Eighty-nine years old, and you know, that man hardly had a gray hair. His hair was just as black . . ."

Minutes later, I went up to look at the corpse. In the off-white satin lining, the face seemed quite waxen. He looked much more like a large doll with a mask that had been sculpted to suggest someone who, indeed, possibly might have been my uncle. The hair was, yes, largely black. But the face seemed wholly sculpted from the makeup on it. Under the dark, pin-striped suit, the chest and arms looked flat as boards. Folded across one another, the hands disappeared under the edge of the lower of the two casket lids.

From the age of eight through sixteen or so, for me to meet someone new was invariably to be asked: "Are you related to Hubert Delany, the Judge . . . ?" While I looked at him, I remembered this—and didn't quite smile at it.

But a moment later, I was surrounded by a bevy of young, twenty and thirty year old cousins, men and women, all of whom were far better tailored than I, half of whom I had never seen before, and the other half of whom I hadn't seen since they were eight, nine, and ten, while a young man in a suit—Hubert T. Delany, grandson of my uncle—was explaining to me: "You know, back when I was at MIT, every time I'd meet somebody new, the first thing they'd ask me is: 'Are you any relation to Samuel Delany, the science fiction writer?'" while the others laughed and nodded, as though it was an experience they all had shared.

Two of the young women were lawyers—also grandchildren of Hubert. And young Hubert had a computer company in Boston. His father, my first cousin, Harry (now a successful surgeon, though I'd grown up calling him "Sonny"), took me aside to explain that the graphics in the "Science Section" of the same *Times* that had carried Uncle Hubert's obituary had been done by young Hubert's Boston company: Delany Graphics. Then he turned to introduce me to his future son-in-law, a resident in surgery at Kings County Hospital (Harry explained), a handsome black kid of about my own complexion, in a very elegant dark suit, with an absolute flurry of black hair sticking out in all directions—the fiance of one of the lawyers I'd just been talking to.

Minutes later, Brother—looking very old and very tall—came in and gave me his hand with its missing fingers to shake. "You know, I got another funeral tomorrow morning at the exact same time?" he told me.

I smiled. I never meet him without rehearsing my mother's antipathy toward him: during the year my father was dying, and he was managing my father's funeral business, it came out that he'd stolen well over fifty-thousand-dollars from the business—for which he was never prosecuted. My mother has always been furious at him. I've never felt the same way—though the money would have meant that I could have gone to a private college, where, possibly, I might actually have done rather well. But that also means I probably would not have become a writer anywhere near as quickly as I did.

Sonny—Dr. Delany, about six years older than I, but physically, I can't help noting, in much better shape—has the reputation of the family historian. He and his tall, slightly darker sister Madalon are both adopted children; they were Aunt Willetta's by a previous marriage. That means they carry no Delany genes. Yet they both look and move and sound like Delanys. Without making a big thing of it, I must say that there really is a kind of Delany style—and both of them have it as much as Logan or Tut or Brother or Peggy or myself. At one point, Sonny was talking to me about Aunt Sadie and Aunt Bessie—Uncle Hubert's two oldest surviving sisters: one is a hundred-one, the other is ninety-nine, and both, he told me, were coming to the funeral tomorrow. (Uncle Hap, an older brother, though still alive, is too infirm to make it.) "Sonny," I said. "Something I've been meaning to ask you. Do you know much about your father's first wife—the poet Clarissa Scott Delany? Perhaps you've seen that two volume biography of Langston Hughes. She and your father are mentioned in there. Hughes was particularly fond of her, and her death—I believe she was only twenty-five years old—was apparently quite upsetting to the entire circle."

Sonny scratched his ear. "Now I know we always had a book of her poems."

"I was wondering if there were any manuscripts—papers, or anything like that?"

"Hey, come on," he said, suddenly taking my shoulder. "Let's go ask Madalon." We started through the crowd.

Madalon was stately, in dusky dark green. (Her sons, for three or four years, used to sublet Marilyn's 105th Street co-op during the summer.)

"Sam is interested in Clarissa Scott—Dad's first wife. You know," he said, turning to me, "she died almost exactly a year after they were married—the day after Dad was confirmed a judge."

And I remembered both my mother and father saying, at various times, "She was really the love of Hubert's life—her death—" from tuberculosis, complicated by leukemia—"was just so tragic!"

Madalon reiterated the point about the book.

Sonny explained again that I was interested in papers and manuscripts. "Try Wellesley," Madalon said. "That's where she went to school." Then she smiled. "The same place I did. If there were any papers, they would have been given to the Wellesley library."

"Thank you!" I said; this interest of mine in the young poet who was, for a year, an aunt of mine by marriage has simmered since my teens. But this was really the first I'd found anything definite about where I might research her. "Thank you. I will."

My plan had been to come for a half an hour, between six-thirty and seven, pay my respects to Aunt Willetta, then leave. But my sister, Peggy, who'd phoned me to tell me the time and place, had assured me she'd be there by seven — so I decided to wait for her. With my coat in my arms against my stomach, I moved to the wall, watching people move about, some familiar, some not. Now and again someone came up to speak to me — sometimes someone I knew, and sometimes someone who thought I was someone I wasn't.

Pretty soon it was ten to eight — and Peggy still hadn't arrived. So, at last, I went up to say goodbye to Aunt Willetta and Aunt Francis, then left.

Back at home, about eleven, Peggy called me. She hadn't been able to get off work till late — much to her consternation. She'd gotten there a little after eight. We'd missed each other by perhaps fifteen minutes. The funeral was to be the next day. Aunt Mary had just called her and told her she would be coming — could Peggy give her a hand?

A problem case, this.

Aunt Mary, the wife of my father's and Uncle Hubert's next oldest brother, Uncle Manross (the first of the Delany children to die, back in fifty-six or fifty-seven), had been a truly brilliant woman. A close friend of James Baldwin, she'd worked with him to establish the Harlem Writers' Guild; she'd taught for years at St. Augustine's, and had gone on frequent trips to Europe — at a time when most people (and certainly most blacks, even of the middle class) did not. She lived at 70 LaSalle Street, in the building right across from where my parents had lived. But in the last decade, as she'd become older and feeble, she'd also become notoriously mentally unstable. For the two or three years before my mother's stroke in the summer of '87, she'd been rather a thorn in my mother's side — as the management of Morningside Gardens knew they were sisters-in-law. And there'd been several incidents where Aunt Mary, now in her eighties, had disappeared into her apartment for days — or had refused to let cleaning people in, or — on one occasion — had gone wandering off, on her walker, and gotten lost on the grounds and had not been able to find her way home, though she was no more than twenty or thirty yards from her front door.

These were all incidents from four or five years back, and it was hard to imagine the situation having gotten any better.

But the previous night Aunt Mary had called Peggy, told her that she would be coming to the funeral using a car service, and would Peggy look out for her and help her from the car into the church.

Peggy was dubious—but had agreed.

The funeral was the next morning, at eleven o'clock, at St. Martin's Church, at a Hundred-Twenty-Second street and Lenox Avenue. It was briskly, cuttingly cold, cloudless, and bright. I got there perhaps quarter to eleven. In her dark coat, blue scarf, and black curly hair, Peggy was waiting in the Church vestibule. I picked up one of the programs for the service, splayed out across a stolid oaken table, and went to talk with her.

She took my arm and leaned toward me. "You'll never guess who's here—" and, when I looked at her questioningly, she said: "Burton!"

At the name, a memory flared as bright as a filmic flashback: some evening in the late spring of nineteen-fifty-seven, lightning whitened the Seventh Avenue window beyond the short, gilt drapes. Then thunder filled up the funeral parlor's entire front office like something solid, wrapping the leather couch and waiting room chairs, surrounding the deco lamps in something thick as fabric so that their orangish light seemed momentarily dimmer; when it died, the rain, splatting on the pains, was loud as gravel. And Burton, a slim young man about twenty-three, with a round, brown face, over a red tie and dark blue suit, stood in the side-office doorway to declare: "Good God, that sounds like someone's gone to war!" Then he laughed with a voice that had a kind of late adolescent honk still in it.

Just then, from the back Chapel, my father called: "Burton—! Burton—Come here, Burton—!"

We looked at each other, then Burton turned to hurry back through the brown veneered doors, and more brown veneered doors, into the long chapel.

In the space I always recall as fundamentally a dark and shadowy taupe (red runner in the aisle, ivory ceiling, stained glass windows off in the distance), light lanced across the gilded backs of rank on rank of folding chairs, painted gold. Across them, I could see that the door to the cellar—usually closed—was now open.

We hurried between the chairs, me wondering if I was to come too, since Dad was calling Burton—

—who swung, now, around the little outset, in which the cellar door was framed, and started down. I paused in the doorway. My father, uncharacteristically in shirt sleeves, was already halfway to the bottom.

Years ago, the cellar, underlying the entire three story building, had been divided into two rooms — the forward one more or less finished, painted yellow, and — for a while — used to display caskets that my father sold. This was the room the stairway decanted into. The back room (I knew) was still raw stone, and in a couple places piles of earth had not yet been dug out; that room housed the boiler for the building; and into it, during my first half dozen years, once a week coal had roared, black and glittering, down a five-yard metal tray, from the truck at street level, to heap between the two shoulder-high (my shoulders: the shoulders of a six-year-old), blackened board walls, beside the round gray furnace — back when, indeed, the building had been heated by coal.

By the time I was seven, my father had stopped selling caskets, though some six were still set up — in double tiers — toward the back of the yellow room. But things were piled on top of them; and the place now was largely used for storage; it had pretty much filled up with junk in the interim.

As I looked down beyond Burton and my father, I saw that the floor was the wrong color, much too black, strangely shiny — and it moved . . . covered, I realized, with three or four inches of water! A shoe box bobbed near the foot of the steps. At other places papers floated. An old, brown enameled filing cabinet, that had been stored down there, was wet to three or four uneven inches above the wavering waterline. And a pile of newspapers by one table leg, perhaps a foot or two high, was completely soaked.

As the three of us stood there on the steps, I heard a grating. At first I thought a wall was coming down. But the wooden trestle under the casket nearest the front gave way — and the casket's tail end crashed into the water, sending a wave along the room that splattered a dark stain a foot up the front wall. Things piled on the casket top slid off, splashing. Then the trestle at the other end collapsed — and the mahogany simply splatted into the flood, sending up spray as high as my father's hand on the rough, plank banister.

The water was not deep enough to float the polished wood. But ripples beat its side, and for moments I thought it was bobbing — that, indeed, the whole house had lost its mooring and was a-wash. It took us all a minute to get our bearings back.

Then Dad and Burton were sitting on the steps, rolling their suit pants up around their knees—my father wore high, dark socks with garters around his shins—and soon they were wading about, the water over the tops of their shoes.

The whole thing made my father a little crazy; I wanted to go down and wade too, of course; and I remember him yelling at me angrily to get out of the water. But I also remember, only minutes later, standing with him and Burton in the second room.

A kind of roaring like a pedal note behind it all had—as I'd entered—grown louder.

The steps up to the iron door opening onto the sidewalk were a waterfall! Foam and froth cascaded and splashed down, as though someone at the dark and dirty top were playing two or three fire hoses into the cellar. Concentric half-rings rilled across the flood.

Burton and my father examined the eight inch cement pedestal on which the new hot-water boiler—put in the previous year—stood. More than half the gray block was submerged. Through an open oval low in the orange enamel, a ring of flame glimmered pale blue below the down curved metal.

"If it gets to that, it's going to be ruined—!" my father all but whispered. "We'll never get it started again."

Burton hazarded, "Perhaps we should turn it off now . . ."

Water filled my sneakers, swirled around my ankles. And later, back in the darkness, I remember looking down at a puppet theater my father had once built for me. In the nether mists of childhood, I'd seen one like it in the Schwarz's *Toy Catalogue* and desperately wanted it for Christmas. But even back then, it had been fifty-five or sixty-five dollars—the equivalent of five or six hundred today. And so my father had taken it upon himself, secretly in the months before Christmas, to build one for me, out of plywood. It had wings and flies; the inside was painted black. The puppets were lowered, on their strings, down through the top. The proscenium was painted green, and there were carefully painted brown scrolls up the sides and over the top—presumably because green and brown paint are what he had in some old cans in the basement. Even so, it was a good deal fancier looking than the one in the catalogue. And for a month or two I'd loved it. But, when it had fallen out of my childish interest, it had gone back to live here in the basement. And now I watched an oily line of dirt slant across its green sides, to be lifted off and deposited still higher up with wavelet after wavelet.

Eventually Peggy came down to sit on the stairs and watch us slog about—in silent sibling jealousy, I'm sure, that she was not allowed to wade.

We got the casket ("Now that's a three hundred dollar casket—and ruined! Just ruined! Careful there, now Burton—and Sam, watch out!" Not that it would ever have been sold; more than likely he would have given it away, possibly for a nominal ten or twenty-five dollars, to someone who could not afford one at all) back up on the saw-horses that served it for catafalque. And soon somebody picked up a wet siding of plywood that somehow had gotten stuck on top of the large drain in the corner: within twenty minutes, the water level had gone down to a simple sheeting of glassy slop across the cement floor.

"I think these shoes," Burton said to me, laughing, but with some real worry in his voice—he had now taken off his jacket and his tie and was in just his shirt sleeves like my father—"are ruined."

I said: "Burton . . . ?" there in the high, stone vestibule of St. Martin's church—was it thirty-four years later? My father, my Uncle Lucius, and my mother's mother had all been buried from this church since then.

"Yes," Peggy said. "He's right inside—he's one of the pallbearers, I think. Go say hello!—I think the bathroom is in back," she added, knowing my overactive bladder.

I went inside the church proper. In the side aisle a half a dozen tall, brown-faced men in dark suits and ties stood together. The tallest—certainly I hadn't seen him since he was twenty-five or so—had a round face and only the slightest of gray at the temples. I came up to him, as he turned to me—"Burton," I said, "I'm Sam Delany. Little Sam."

His frown became a smile. "—Hi, *there!*" in a voice which sounded as though, years ago, he might had swallowed a voice like Burton's that now was just an echo to his own much deeper baritone. "Little Sam . . . !"

He shook my hand and clapped me on the shoulder. Then he added —it didn't seem gratuitous at the time—"Your father gave us some good training!"

We enthused at one another. Then, when he turned away to say something to one of the other men, I went up to the front of the church to take another look at Uncle Hubert in his coffin — the facial make-up registered with the same order of unreality with which it had struck me last night — then went back out to join Peggy.

Now we began to talk about the Aunt Mary problem — if there was to be one. It ended with my, first, going to call Aunt Mary to see if she'd left yet. There was no answer on her phone; so I assumed she had. Then Peggy and I waited on the church steps, looking up and down the street. Things got a bit complicated when a funeral car pulled up and my cousin, Virginia Murphy, got out, followed by Aunt Sadie and Aunt Bessie. There was, of course, a bustle around them. I wanted just to give the two old women my love and a kiss, and otherwise stay back — but then someone was saying to me, "Sam, you go into the church with Aunt Sadie."

And I was walking Aunt Sadie, in her dark coat and small black pill-box hat, up the street to the church steps.

My mother's mother lived till a hundred-two; and Aunt Sadie is currently a hundred-one. Yet the difference between them is total. Once she was 86, my grandmother, though she did housework into her mid-nineties, never left my mother's apartment again — not even to go outside and sit in the sun (except when, at 93, she broke her hip and went into the hospital for two weeks); Aunt Sadie and Aunt Bessie both go to yoga classes (a few years ago they were on TV). But where grandma was dumpy, terribly good hearted, but opinionated and timid, both Sadie and Bessie are like slender, benevolent hawks. Aunt Sadie had no trouble at all with the steps, and as we were walking down the aisle, I said to her: "Well, young lady, I guess that yoga isn't such a bad idea after all!"

She turned to me and laughed full out.

Bessie, who was a dentist as well as a Greek teacher, and is now a clear-eyed ninety-nine, chattered on behind us, "Is that Little Sam up there — oh, dear me. With all that hair on his face? Well, isn't that . . . Oh, now don't let me say anything! Well, now, this is Elie's boy? Oh, and Mark — of course I recognize you, son . . . !"

Once I handed Aunt Sadie in to her pew, with the secondary family (as funeral directors call it), I rushed back up the aisle — practically to run into Brother, who, once again, gave me his fingerless hand to shake and who, in a replay of our meeting last night, repeated: "Hello, there, Sam—do you know I have another funeral the same time as this, at a church just six blocks away?" I nodded, said hello, but hurried out to the church steps again to look for Aunt Mary.

No more than a minute later, I saw her, coming down the cold, cold street, on her walker. I ran up to meet her. Her face was more gray than brown, with a texture like the inside of certain cardboard egg containers. She wore an old and rather tatty coat, pale green, and inch or two of its hem torn and hanging. She only wore one glove, a moleskin affair, losing the seam along the inside of the forefinger. Leaning on the walker's aluminum bar, she took small but constant steps.

"Hello, Aunt Mary! You got here. Peggy and I were just beginning to wonder—"

"Sam, is that you? Oh, it was awfully nice of you to come here and meet me like this. Where is my other glove? Now I know I had it in my purse—I've got my purse? Oh, good lord, now if I lost that, I'd really be in some trouble, wouldn't I—"

"You've got it right there, Aunt Mary. Let's go on inside, and we can look for the glove once you get out of this cold."

"Oh, it *is* cold this morning—Whew, it certainly is!" And we continued together to the steps, both of us, I suspect, concentrating too much on the mechanics of her movement really to feel it.

I took the walker and put it on the top step, then helped her up. On the one hand, I was mildly shocked to see the shabbiness this globe-hopping woman who spoke French and German and Spanish and Italian had come to; but, though the sky was glass blue and there was little wind, shock was dulled by the veil of coldness itself and my anxiousness to get her inside all that gray-black stone, where it would be warmer.

Once we got settled together in a pew with Peggy, I noticed a young man in the pew ahead. Slim and with black hair, he could have easily been (I fancied) my handsome younger brother, if I'd had one. But even as I noticed him, he turned to speak to me. "Excuse me, Sam—you probably don't remember me. I'm Logan—" who, though I wouldn't have remembered him, true, I recalled now that I'd last seen when Marilyn and I, days after our marriage, had gone to visit my Uncle Hubert at Greenwood Lake, and Little Logan—one of the more recent sons of my Uncle Lucius's son, Big Logan—was a somewhat fleshy, but very pleasant, eleven-year-old. Now, thirty years later, in his dark suit, as he leaned over to speak to me, I told him: "Logan, of course I remember you. What are you doing now?"

"I work on Wall Street," he confided. "I have a son, Gavin—you once did a book called *Empire*?"

"That's right," I said. "It was a big comic book, with Howard Chaykin."

"Ah!" Logan said, as though a mystery had been explained. "Yes, Gavin's very interested in comic books. He wanted me to . . . well, ask you about that book—"

He seemed a little uncomfortable. So I decided to make things easier for him. "Would he like a copy? I could certainly send him one. I have a few of them still lying around."

"*Would* you?" He seemed relieved—I hope because a somewhat embarrassing mission had been rendered a bit easier to perform. "He'd really appreciate that. He's twelve," he added.

"Certainly," I said. I opened my notebook to put down his address. (A draft of my review of Byatt[11] was tucked into the back.) "By the way, Logan, how old are you now?"

"Forty-one," he said.

I'd have guessed thirty-one. But then, with a twelve-year-old son, I suppose—

"I have another friend," he went on. "He's also a great fan of yours. His name is Bob Stanford. He's someone I work with."

"Perhaps if you had a book of yours you might send him, too—with an autograph. Or even just a piece of paper with an autograph he could paste in to a book of yours he already owns. Probably not a comic book, though—"

"Certainly," I told him. "Just put his address down too."

"Well, if you sent it in care of me, I could see that he got it . . ."

Was I making it easier for him, I wondered, or was I just being self-

---

11. "Antonio Byatt's *Possession: A Romance,*" in *Shorter Views: Queer Thoughts and the Politics of the Paraliterary,* by Samuel R. Delany (Hanover, NH: University of New England Press for Wesleyan University Press, 1999). The review was finished in 1990.

important and grandiose. One wonders what tale he might have taken home from the encounter. But that, of course, I'll probably never know.

A moment after he finished writing, the funeral itself began.

My impression of the previous evening's gathering on St. Nicholas Avenue had been by-and-large pleasant. But as the funeral itself went on, I found myself feeling oddly intimidated.

It was a strange feeling—not that there was anything out of place in the service.

The Minister explained that Uncle Hubert had been good friends with his own father, late a minister here at St. Martin's, and that Uncle Hubert had regularly served as lay reader during the Wednesday night services here at the church for some eight or nine years, during the fifties. No mention was made of his last twenty years' infirmity: indeed, all spoke of him as if it *were* twenty years ago and Hubert's death had come just at the beginning of his incapacity, rather than at the end of so long and disturbing an affliction.

The first of the five eulogists was Neal MacDougal, who had, incidentally, been my parents' lawyer, and whose daughters, Mary and Connie, went to Dalton with me and with whom I played as a child in the black social club, the Jack and Jill of America. An easy speaking and articulate man in his healthy seventies now, a black man with a complexion like pulp paper when it gets very old, he recounted: When Neal was a grade school student in New York, my Uncle—age twenty, and only a couple of years out of North Carolina—was Neal's Fifth Grade teacher; Neal explained Uncle Hubert's gentle but effective way of maintaining discipline among the young black schoolboys (I gather it was an all boys' school), by talking to them, straightforwardly and honestly, about what they could expect socially ahead of them, as young Negro men going out into a world of white power.

Some fifteen or so years later, Neal recounted, when Neal himself was a young lawyer and Hubert was now a judge, Hubert phoned Neal and asked him to represent, for no fee, a poor black family coming before the bench.

Neal accepted the assignment.

When he came to the judge's chambers, Uncle Hubert passed on to him the relevant papers, which included the reports to the New York

City Welfare Department on the family. Uncle Hubert handed these over to Neal, with the exhortation to look at *all* aspects of the papers *very* carefully. Neal examined the papers there, and, by his own account, all seemed to be in order — except that, in the upper right hand corner, there was a strange pencil mark that he didn't understand.

He brought it to Uncle Hubert's attention, who nodded and simply said: "Yes, that's one of the things that I'm concerned about, too."

In the hearing, Neal questioned the social worker who had filled out the forms. The young woman became rather upset. But, finally, it came out that this mark was a mark that all the social workers put on the forms of black families to let the office know that, indeed, these clients *were* black; forms bearing this mark were then routed through an entirely different — and much inferior — set of programs. But the exposure of this practice, in the New York City Welfare Department in the late thirties, was one of the first cases by which Uncle Hubert began to garner his reputation as a fiery advocate of Civil Rights — at a time when many such rights were *not* vouchsafed by the land's law.

Now Sonny spoke — and talked about his father's belief in the family and in honesty and right. He read a condolence letter from the city's Mayor Dinkins to Aunt Willetta, praising Uncle Hubert's work during his judgeship tenure.

Next to speak was young Hubert, Sonny's son. Once again, I found myself struck by how clearly and strongly Sonny and his children were so definitely Delanys — in their movements, in their voices, and in their attitudes, even though there was no genetic connection between us. (This, of course, was the aspect of the Delanys that had inspired my portrait of the Dyeths in *Stars in My Pocket Like Grains of Sand*. It was warming to see it so evident again, here.) Young Hubert recounted that, as a child, he'd first been told that his grandfather was his "Pop's pop," and so therefore had started calling Uncle Hubert by the childish nickname "Pop-pop" — which was finally taken over by all the other grandchildren. One of Hubert's earliest memories of Pop-pop was coming in to see him in his house.

From his big chair, Pop-pop had asked: "What's your name, boy?"

(How easy it is, from my own store of memories, to hear Uncle Hubert asking such a question!)

Young Hubert had answered: "Hubert T. Delany, sir."

"And don't you ever forget it!" Pop-pop had shot back.

The two young women lawyers next came to speak of Pop-pop's legacy as a lawyer to them. One read out the moving statement Uncle Hubert had made shortly after not being reappointed as a judge by Mayor Wagner: in it, he affirmed his belief in America and his mission to set up a condition of equality between blacks and whites by the pursuit of truth. It would be very easy for me to make such a statement my motto today. Indeed, it left me feeling my uncle was quite a rhetorician. The next granddaughter told how much her knowledge of Pop-pop's political career had meant to her during her own law-school days.

Finally, from just in front of us, Logan was called up to the pulpit to read a resolution from the New York City YMCAs, attesting to the help that Uncle Hubert had given to New York youth during his active years.

Then, a young woman, with dark face and veiled white hat, sang, extraordinarily well, two of my Uncle's favorite spirituals: "There Is a Balm in Gilead," and "Every Time I Feel the Spirit" — working against, I really must mention, the worst church organists I believe I've *ever* heard!

The sense of intimidation I spoke of, however, grew with my own growing realization that mine — at least the Delany half — is an extremely powerful family. There is a great deal of money in that family — and it is not mine.

Through various hymns and various preachments, through standings and sittings and the rustling of prayer book and hymnal pages, I recalled the moment, shortly after my marriage to Marilyn, when, sitting in our empty apartment on East Sixth Street in the red armchair newly down from her mother's, I'd articulately realized that, if I followed the path of least resistance, without any trying at all I would slide into a good job, a solid career, and a fair amount of material success — and decided, at that moment of that realization, that I would instead pursue my talents — and thus, most likely, bypass precisely that particular order of success.

And, thirty-years later, it is what I have done.

The gamble was for fame — and, on that count, I have been (modestly) successful. To my young cousins, I *am* the famous Delany. But I hadn't foreseen the material consequences of being a pudgy, bushy-bearded man, just shy of fifty, in mismatched shoes, pants, and jacket, with a knitted watchcap and an overcoat gone shiny at the shoulders — amidst these numerous tri-partite generations of lawyers and doctors and Wall-Street brokers, a-sea in the attendant signs (Aunt Mary not withstanding) of their wealth. I found myself feeling really uncomfortable — and amused at the discomfort.

But most people who die in New York City don't get quarter-page obituaries in the *Times*. Most people who die in New York City don't have three-page condolence letters from the Mayor read out at their funerals. I felt like the successful peasant farmer who'd wormed an invitation to an aristocratic gathering and who was now sweatingly uncomfortable for having come, like a not very sympathetic character out of a Balzac novel. Yes, I was able to smile at the feeling — but that didn't *stop* it!

The final hymn started; the pallbearers lined up at either side of the aisle's head — Burton, so familiar and so strange, among them. Other bearers included young Hubert and Sonny's prospective surgeon son-in-law, with his very fine suit and *all* his hair! The casket, closed now, moved up the aisle between. The immediate family filed out, Aunt Willetta holding Madalon's hand, Sonny solicitous of them both. Aunt Sadie and Aunt Bessie, and the others of the secondary family followed. Peggy and I came with Aunt Mary, a considerable space between her walker and the dark coated backs just ahead of us.

The heat of the church fell away in the dark, stony vestibule.

Outside, the cars were pulling up to take people to the cemetery; from the burial, people were going back to Sonny's and Barbara's house in New Rochelle for a gathering. Peggy was going there. But Aunt Mary and I were not — I had reams of work to do back at home.

At my suggestion, Aunt Mary and I moved toward the corner. I had no idea what her service car looked like. While we were waiting, Logan drove up in his very shiny, very blue car and leaned out the window to ask if we needed a lift. I smiled and told him no, we were just waiting for her car to pick her up.

But even before the first of the cars began to leave for the cemetery, beside the milling black veils and black coats, pulling up to the corner was a red van — with the name of the transportation company that Aunt

THE NEW YORK TIMES **OBITUARIES** MONDAY, DECEMBER 31, 1990

Dec 31st, 1990

Hubert T. Delany, 89, Ex-Judge And Civil Rights Advocate, Dies

By GEORGE JAMES

The New York Times, 1968

Hubert T. Delany

Hubert T. Delany, a justice in the New York City Domestic Relations Court from 1942 to 1955 and an early civil rights advocate, died on Friday at Presbyterian Hospital in Manhattan, where he lived. He was 89 years old.

He died of heart disease, his son, Dr. Harry M. Delany, said.

Justice Delany, a Republican, was appointed to family court by Mayor Fiorello H. La Guardia after serving

Praised for his humanity in family court.

for five years as an assistant United States Attorney in the criminal division and as a member of New York City's Tax Commission for eight years.

Admirers praised the judge for understanding, independence and humanity in his rulings on delicate family issues, but detractors assailed some decisions as too permissive and liberal.

Wagner Denied Reappointment

In 1955, Mayor Robert F. Wagner, a Democrat, denied him reappointment for what the Mayor called his reportedly "left-wing views." Mr. Wagner declined to elaborate, except to say that he was not challenging the judge's patriotism. An article in The New York Times said that Mr. Delany had been rejected because he was accused of links with left-wing and pro-Communist groups.

A Times editorial supporting his reappointment said in part: "As far as we are aware, Mr. Delany has been offered no chance to disprove or to answer these allegations. Furthermore, his performance as a judge has received high praise from groups best fitted to know, including the Association of the Bar of the City of New York."

The former justice attributed the

Mayor's action to his speaking out for civil rights and against second-class citizenship. Many public figures and other newspapers defended his rulings and his appeals for wider civil rights and liberties for blacks and other minorities. In later decades, he was appointed to lead many New York State and city panels battling for improved and integrated housing, education and health benefits.

Mr. Delany had been a longtime board member of the National Association for the Advancement of Colored People and its Legal Defense and Educational Fund, the National Urban League, the 135th Street branch of the Y.M.C.A., Talladega College in Alabama, the Episcopal Diocese of New York and the alumni association of City College. He had a private law practice for many years.

Son of Former Slave

Hubert Thomas Delany was born in Raleigh, N.C. His father, Henry B. Delany, was a former slave who became a suffragan bishop of the Episcopal Church; his mother, Nanny J. Delany, was a longtime teacher in St. Augustine's College in Raleigh, where he received his early education.

He graduated from the City College of New York in 1923 and New York University Law School in 1926. During his schooling, he worked at tobacco farms in Connecticut, as a redcap at Pennsylvania Station and as a teacher in Harlem elementary schools.

In 1929, Mr. Delany ran for a House seat from Manhattan's 21st District, which included much of Harlem and Washington Heights, but he was trounced, but he struck up an abiding friendship with Mr. La Guardia.

Surviving, besides his son, who lives in Mount Vernon, N.Y., are his wife, Willetta; a daughter, Dr. Madelon Stent of the Bronx; three sisters, Sadie and Bessie, both of Mount Vernon, and Laura Murrell of Oakland, Calif.; a brother, Henry, of Mount Vernon; six grandchildren, and two great-grandchildren.

SRD: It intrigues me that, in the obituary above, no mention occurs of the degenerative brain disease never given a name, which left Hubert T. Delany all but a vegetable for 30 years, during which he was taken care of at home by his wife, Willeta, and visiting nurses, and unable to leave the house. (I never heard any mention of Alzheimer's.) At this date, I have seen no mention of this condition anywhere online. This is part of the nation's extremely strange and unealthy attitude toward death and the unknown in general.

Obituary for Hubert T. Delany, New York Times, *December 31, 1990.*

Mary had given me. The attendant, in his heavy red down jacket and visored cap with corduroy ear muffs, was just climbing out. As he opened the side and put down the stool, I realized this was a transportation service specifically *for* the elderly; and I felt a surge of relief.

We got Aunt Mary inside; a hug, a good bye, a wish for a good trip home—and moments later, the van was pulling away across Lenox, back toward Morningside Gardens. And I continued up the broad avenue, wide and clear as some concrete football field, to take the subway at 125th Street.

On the train, I sat, going over my review of *Possession* for the fifteenth or the twenty-fifth time to unsettle and move out those unsettling feelings, while I road downtown—and almost missed my change at 96th Street.

Later that night, about eleven, when she got home to Brooklyn, Peggy phoned me again.

"You know," she said, "it was really funny. I felt rather intimidated by the whole thing—I mean, when I got to Sonny and Barbara's, well . . . they don't live in a house, really. They live in a mansion! I'm not kidding, it's like some sort of castle!" (Shortly after Marilyn and I were married, we'd gone to dinner with Barbara and Sonny in their then West-side apartment; even back then, it now seems to me, it had been possible to judge the social trajectory at which they were moving.) "Of course, everybody was as warm and friendly as they could be—and of course everyone asked after you, and was so sorry you couldn't make it. But for the first few minutes, I really found myself asking, what in the world I was *doing* there. I really felt intimidated—" she said, repeating the word I'd been using to myself back at the funeral. "This is a very high powered family we come from. It was enough to make you uncomfortable. Though, finally, I'm glad I went."

Which, I suppose, is the way I feel, too.

On Christmas Eve I thought of you—and how, so often, I'd be able to find time to drop you a line. But, this year, things were more hectic. I thought of you, too, on the 14th—Iva's birthday.

For a while there, it seemed to have become a tradition to write to you while her friends partied in the other room. But Iva—who was seventeen this year—had had her party on New Year's Eve. So for the birthday day itself, Dennis and I took her and her school friend Yves out to Bazzini's Restaurant (an Italian restaurant Iva likes a lot), where, in our little booth, over garlic bread and pasta, Dennis and I gave her our presents: from me, earrings, from Dennis, a leather pouch.

And my lovely, long-haired daughter—bending to put her new jet and silver earrings on, while Yves, cried: "Oh, they're lovely! " — was a perfect lady!

One must speak of the War.

On March 15th, the day Bush had set as the deadline for Hussein, Don Keller called to say that the proofs of the *Possession* review were in, and I could come down to William Morrow (where Don works as David Hartwell's assistant) and proof them.

Don is a rather interesting fellow. An extremely energetic and intelligent fan, he helped publish the "Women in Science Fiction Symposium," with Jeff Smith, back in '75, and he is half of Serconia Press (who did *The Straits of Messina*); also he is the typesetter who set *Starboard Wine*, lo these many years ago. Recently, he's decided to make a way for himself in professional, New York publishing — and up and moved here from Seattle. With his early experience as a printer (and as an omnivorous reader — much like yourself), he has quite an interesting take on most things. Currently in his late thirties, he's an extraordinarily smallish man, thin, with glasses, and not suited to the slacks and ties that he wears; really, he's rather messy — with long hair that, if I were trying to make *my* way in publishing, I would probably cut. Still, I'm terribly fond of him — and he is terribly bright.

The first surprise for me when I reached the office (Howard, the black guy who — today — heads the mailroom, and who worked there when I was temping at Morrow, five or so years back, rolled the mail cart by me, with a big, "Well, hello, Chip!"), was that David had put my review on the *first* page! I was more than a bit dubious — I'd had a lot of feature exposure on the first page this last year. And, usually, reviews were not first page material. I didn't want it to look as if I were getting special treatment. But, later, David explained that a feature article they'd been expecting to come back with revisions hadn't materialized. Mine was a major review of a prize-winning book; so . . .

When I finished with David and Don, I headed uptown.

I decided to walk through the Forty-Second street area — because I enjoy its insistent sleaziness — and ran into Dennis — in his gray watch cap, gray jacket, and gray sweatpants — wandering down Eighth Avenue, just in front of the Capri Theater. He'd gotten tired of 72nd Street, his usual place for hanging out and gabbing with old street friends, so had come down here.

We decided to take the bus home together.

As soon as we got on, to sit toward the back, the driver announced that the bus had already been re-routed, and that it would be rerouted once again when we got to 72nd Street—mumblings among the passengers—because of the demonstrations, the driver explained.

"What demonstrations?" Dennis asked me.

"It must be a peace demonstrations," I told him. "This is the fifteenth—the end of Bush's waiting period."

When we reached 72nd Street, there were hundreds of people crowding the waist-high iron pickets around Needle Park (Verdi Square, on Manhattan's official map), spilling across Broadway to the base of the great glass windows of the M&C Tape, CD, and Record Store. Many of the people held white candles, glimmering and thrust through squares of cardboard or paper to catch the wax. A platform with a couple of loudspeakers above it on metal scaffolding was visible somewhere over the heads of the crowd. For the sixth time, the driver announced: "This bus will *not* be continuing up Broadway, but will go up Amsterdam. It will return to Broadway at 96th Street. Once again, this bus will not be continuing up Broadway—"

"Come on, Dennis," I said. "Let's get off and see what's going on."

"What do you wanna *see*?" Dennis asked, following me to the door, as the bus pulled up to the stop at the north-east corner of Amsterdam and 72nd.

"The demonstration!" and touched the yellow strip that, on that bus thankfully was still working: the doors swing back; and I hurried—with painful knees and—trying to hold on to the upright post as I climbed down—aching shoulders, out into the chill and damp, with Dennis loping along behind me.

There wasn't, alas, much to see, after all.

We were handed a dozen odd leaflets and flyers. We worked our way up through the crowd, which was, apparently, gathering for a march uptown.

"I bet," Dennis kept saying, "that them Anti-War protests for Vietnam were a whole lot bigger than this! This probably ain't no protest at all, compared to them, I bet!"

"Dennis," I said, "this is pretty big. There're probably about three or four thousand people here."

"But I bet the Vietnam ones were bigger—I never saw them. I was just a kid. But I bet they were."

"Well," I said, "they've got to start somewhere."

So, with Dennis spectacularly unimpressed, we worked our way uptown, while people moved about us with their candles, or passed out protests leaflets in the early evening dark. Around us, there was much talk of other marches around the city—especially a much larger one down at the UN. Somehow the loudspeakers were particularly boomingly muzzy—so that, after *not* hearing the first five minutes of an impassioned speech from the platform, we pulled free of the crowd and made our way north—keeping a block ahead of them, who, now, with their candles, were surging, like a wave headed by luminous, fiery froth behind us, up Broadway.

Back home, Dennis brought his radio into the kitchen, and we listened to WINS News for about an hour, while I cooked.

I went to bed just after 9:30 pm—and woke, beside a snoring Dennis—moments after 3:15 am. I got up, out in the kitchen made myself a hot chocolate, and, taking it into the dining room, sat down in my underwear at the cluttered, round oak table, and read the first 75 pages of Simmons's Hugo winning SF novel *Hyperion*. My sense was that, so far, I was reading a totally mindless and incompetently written book. But perhaps it would turn into something, in another couple of hundred pages.

Once, getting up to stretch, I walked through the arch into the living room, and found a book, still in its book mailer, on the couch—Senior Bertram, who often collects packages for me, must have brought it up and given it to Dennis after I'd gone to sleep. It was Ray Monk's biography, *Wittgenstein*, that Adam Bellow (Saul Bellow's son) had sent me from Macmillan Free Press—with a very nice note.

In my notebook, I jotted down a reminder to send Adam a thank note.

Also noted down that I still had to send Gavin Delany a copy of *Empire* (with a copy of *Triton* for Bob Stanford), as I'd promised Logan back at the funeral. In my journal, I wrote out my account of the day and rubber cemented in the first of a sampling of the flyers we'd been handed back at the demonstration.

It now was a handful of hours past Bush's midnight deadline, and the city still seemed comparatively quiet. As I was writing, I heard a noise down the corridor and glanced up—

Dennis was getting up, sleepily, to wander down the hall to the bathroom: "What are you doing up at this ungodly hour . . . ?" he mumbled— and I used his momentary absence to dash into the cluttered bedroom, turn on the light by the bed, and retrieve a dispenser of Scotchtape I knew was there, so I could go on taping in my flyer samples.

Tom Disch had been scheduled to speak at the New York Public Library earlier that evening; vaguely I'd been planning to go. But finally I'd stayed home—and gone to bed. David Hartwell, I know, had gone. I hoped he'd get Tom's lecture for NYRSF, if just so I could get a chance to read it.

I was scheduled to lecture at the Library the following week, closing out their SF series. (It had begun with Roger Zelazny, the previous week. But I'd missed that, too.) In a rare and uncharacteristic moment of organization, I'd actually completed my own lecture the previous week —right after I'd first finished the Byatt piece. Remembering this, as I'd finally begun to get tired (it was now 5:00 in the morning), I felt rather good. So, when Dennis returned from the bathroom, I went in, got in beside him, and we went back to sleep.

The next day (the 16th), I subwayed down to Tor Books, saw Big Del Gaizo Fellow (who's becoming quite involved with the managing editor, Maria Malili—something of a Kitty [his last girlfriend—in a relation that came to (for him) an emotionally catastrophic end] look-alike. Does this bode well or no . . . ?), then went out to lunch with David H[artwell] to a pleasant and homey place, called Michael's. We talked about everything from Christina Sedgwick (see the most recent issue of *Science Fiction Studies*) to David's current divorce from Pat, to the *New York Review of Science Fiction*, to Dan Simmons. While we were at Michael's, we ran into Claire Eddy (another Tor editor she, and wife of my lawyer, David Kogelman, who looks, at this moment, as if she is at least 47 months pregnant); she was taking to lunch sf author Rebecca Orr — who'd stopped in New York on her way to Washington to research an alternate history novel . . . concerned with the Great War and the Ottoman Empire, I believe.

Back home, there was a phone message from Iva that she was spending the night at her school friend Meredith's.

And, a moment after I finished playing it back, a phone call from Ellen Datlow at *Omni* — would I consider doing a short-short for them? I was feeling very good about work in general, so I said yes. She was asking six writers all to do short-shorts (c. 1,500 words) around a single illustration. I suggested that I drop in the next day, on my way down to the Museum of Modern Art to meet Barbara and pick up a copy of it.

Sure, she said.

At about four, I got under the covers to lay down for what I assumed would be an hour — and immediately fell out. I vaguely recall Dennis coming in to tell me it was five, and I said something like, yes, yes, we'd eat in just a little while as soon as I got up.

What I did, of course, was fall out again — and sleep through the first hour of the War.

The sound of the phone roused me — and Dennis doesn't usually like to deal with phone messages. So, in just my undershirt, I got up and more or less staggered into the dining room (vaguely aware of Dennis, sitting on the living room floor, cross-legged, watching his little portable TV), to pick up the phone.

It was Professor Levine, calling from Amherst, who said: "Hello, Chip — did you know we've been at war for the last hour — since about seven o'clock?"

"Dear God!" I said. "No . . . ?"

It seems that Dennis had recorded the first half hour of it for me, figuring I'd want to hear it when I woke up!

We watched the coverage up through President Bush's nine-o'clock homily: myself, I thought it was pretty pale.

The coverage of the protests seemed moderately adequate, however.

After the president spoke, I got into my clothes and Dennis and I went downstairs to the Silk Road for an uneasy Chinese dinner. (They

serve free wine—and, bless them, lots of it.) My own feelings: intellectually I know this is an appalling move. Still, there is some relief in that,
since we have done it, we seem to have at least started off doing it right.
But I was afraid that we would probably end up paying for it, in some
way that we cannot yet even frame—in international Karma as it were.

❖

The next morning (17th), coming back from breakfast at the Galaxy
Deli, I stopped to look at a forlorn, yellow and black sticker someone
had recently pasted on the dark green circuit box on the corner lamp-
post at 81st Street and Amsterdam. It said: "My New Year's Resolution:
No War in the Gulf."

At about twelve-thirty, I took off to meet Barbara at MOMA—planning to stop at the *Omni* offices *en route*. The sky was extraordinary that
day: in the contracting V of buildings, first down Amsterdam Avenue,
and a few moments later, down Broadway, the clouds were a richly tex-
tured and tarnished aluminum, lit from an odd angle that cast a kind of
sourceless silver into the streets—the sort of day that painters, seeking
their north-light, yearn for. The bits of sky between were almost indigo;
and every object in the city with yellows or red or earths in it glowed
with an inner light because of it.

At the Broadway bus-stop, in front of Burger King, I saw Carol Nixon,
with her short blond hair and her dark cloth coat; she saw me, smiled,
but looked rather limp.

"Hi, there!" I said. "How are you doing?"

She shook her head as I came over to her. "I don't know—really."

"How do you like our new war?"

Just then, the bus pulled up, and as we got on and we took a seat
together, she said: "That's what I mean—I really don't know if I can take
this. I mean, when your personal life isn't going very well, then something like this starts . . . well, it can throw you for a loop. I've just been in
a state, all last night and today."

I nodded. Often a charming and wonderfully outgoing woman, now
she looked quite haggard. "I've got two sons," she went on, looking
off with a kind of worried air. "Both of them are draft age—really, this
hasn't been a good day for me at all. I'm going to see a friend of mine
now—in the hospital—he's sixty-nine years old, and I've been sublet-

ting my apartment from him for the last five years. He's got AIDS. And when he dies, I haven't any idea *what*'s going to happen to me with the landlord . . ." She sighed, deeply.

For a moment, I got the impression that she was on the edge of tears.

So I put my arm around her and gave her a squeeze. Much more quietly than I'd started out, we talked a while more—really, I listened to her, mostly—till we reached 65th Street; then I said good-bye and got off (knees, shoulders) before the red neon stripping in the windows of Tower Records. But I was more than a little sobered, when I walked up to the entrance at 1965. When people's personal lives are in a mess, public disasters seem to enlarge the personal and make it cover the world. As I went in to the lobby, I found myself remembering Rennie Perkins's suicide so many years ago, and its relation to Robert Kennedy's assassination.

Upstairs, in the *Omni* offices Ellen was out. But her assistant, Robert Killheffer, took me in and showed me a repro of the picture (a woman, in a remarkably bland landscape, sitting before some pictures on a table, one of which is an SF version of Vermeer's "Woman at the Window"), then gave me a rather dim Polaroid of it. By the time I was on the subway, I'd all but written my short-short in my head:

A mini-gimmick time-travel story.

Now it's just a matter of finding time to put it down on paper.

Barbara Wise and I were scheduled to see the first two installments of Edgar Reitz's fifteen-hour-forty minute German epic *Heimat*. The museum was screening it over the next four days. After speaking with Carol, the idea of going to such an excessive art work on the first full day of war seemed a bit frivolous; but what to do . . .

At the museum, Barbara was just coming from lunch with Harriet Bee, and we all enthused to each other in the museum lobby and exchanged a message to and from Guy Davenport (whom Harriet is editing). Then down to the basement of MOMA, where, in the front row of the Roy and Niuta Titus Theater, we spent five hours sitting two seats away from dark-haired, maroon sweatered Susan Sontag—who, though we share both Professor Levine and Walter Abish as very good mutual friends, was—*surrounded* by the young couple she was with—simply unapproachable.

[83]

And stayed so, I might add, for all four days of the film's lengthy showings.

Heimat ("Homeland") itself is quite lovely, drifting poetically (the only word) from black-and-white to color and back. Its message is that the Germans really are nice people after all—even if they're not too hot on Gypsies and Jews. And though one doesn't question the message itself, it's impossible for me to see (another) such film without asking: Well, why does someone want to make this film again (and, in this case, at such length) *this* time?

As far as I could tell, over the four days, Barbara actually slept through less than a third of it—which was pretty good.

All in all, in the way of adult soap opera, it was quite pleasant. One of the things that an art work of that length does—Wagner's *Ring*, Ray's *Pather Panchali* (the whole trilogy), Syberberg's *Parsifal* or *Our Hitler*, Musil's *Mann ohne Eigenschaften*, or Proust's *Recherche*—is start the audience off in a state of non-expectation. One knows it is going to go on all-but-forever, so one relaxes oneself and does not even *look* for moments suggesting closure for the first day or two or three of the experience. Then, by the time one has reached the last days, not looking for closure has become a habit—which makes those closing gestures, when they fall, fall with the resonance of a wholly new and other esthetic effect.

I have many quibbles with the film, here and there. Perhaps the largest is the unnecessary carnival scene that closes things out and that makes the real resolution, Old Glasisch's dying dream, seem like a pale grace note, rather than a real conclusion—which it would have been if it had come on just an ordinary, chill evening in the little Hunsrück town. The dream, in which Glasisch, about to die himself, meets all his dead friends, is a quiet note in the carnival's confusion—rather than a heightened note in the intense and generally unrelenting quietness of the little town where, carnivals aside, nothing ever really happens.

Essentially, what Reitz gives us is the reintensified climax to a *short* film—not the necessarily grave and stately climax to the epic film he's actually made.

It's a case of heaping strangeness on strangeness . . . and in a film that almost rigorously eschews the strange for the ordinary, it's really one "strangeness" too many.

Oh, well.

But, with both my esthetic and ideological quibbles, I still liked it . . .

While missiles fell in Haifa and Tel Aviv and in Saudi Arabia . . .

And whatever faith I had in the initial rightness of the war move eroded . . .

A truly fine thing—Mark Gawron showed up in New York, for his wedding party: he recently married his lovely Jenny. And Jenny's relatives (the family of my Dalton friend, Wendy Osserman), threw a wonderful reception for them. I got a whole Sunday morning to talk and chat with Mark, about life, literature, and his new novel—just finished, and waiting for a response from David at Morrow.

It really should be the narrative jewel of this letter.

But, like all the good things in the world, it probably must remain a private wonder.

The night before Dennis and I took the bus up here, back to Amherst, on the evening of Tuesday, January 22, I gave my lecture at the New York Public Library: "Science, Fiction, and the Public Library." Imagine a vast, vaulted hall, with gilt and columns and mosaics and an audience of about a hundred twenty-five (bottle necked in the vestibule outside, due to the security check going on because of the war: the Public Library is a prime target for terrorist attacks). My old downstairs neighbor, Mrs. Jackson (Ann), brought my sister in from Brooklyn to hear me speak —as a surprise to us both. As well, about ten old friends of my mother's showed up; and Eunice Weed—an old friend of Bernie Kay's—was also there. She told me that Big Iva, after whom my Iva's named, is now in a nursing home in New Hampshire. That was kind of a shock. But, since Bernie's death, back in '82, it hasn't been an easy eight years for her.

The meat of my lecture was cannibalized from an interview I did years ago out in Lawrence, Kansas, but the frame was written for the occasion.

You may recognize some of that material from an old letter to you and Pep—I'll make a copy and send it on.

A few weeks before, I'd watched an English actress "perform" Virginia Wolfe's *A Room of One's Own* on Masterpiece Theater over PBS—it

[85]

was stunning! Inspired by that, I decided: why not give a truly histrionic reading of my lecture, complete with gestures and much emotional emphasis and changes in tone. I was a little leery—but, apparently, it worked.

While I was delivering it, I noticed that Barbara Wise and John Del Gaizo were there, sitting next to one another, toward the back of the audience. With his new black beard, Big Del Gaizo Fellow sat forward, eager and attentive through the whole thing. And Barbara, I noticed after a while, was sleeping—but she does (at the theater and at movies, these days) that a lot.

When, after the question session, while much applause still rang out in the hall and I was coming off the platform, David Cronin (who runs the library's Public Education Program, under whose auspices I was lecturing) whispered to me: "My—that was elegant!"

Afterwards, when, with David Hartwell and Kathryn Cramer (along with Terry Bisson), I went out for drinks, David kept on saying: "Really, Chip, you know you were never a dull speaker. But I guess the last couple of years' teaching experience has really improved your public delivery—that was *very* good!"

Which is funny, since it's hardly the teaching: any improvement in my delivery must be blamed on the nameless actress who portrayed Mrs. Wolfe on PBS.

Many thanks for your letter of January 2nd, Bob! I do appreciate your reassuring me about those troubling thoughts I was having, inspired by Ms. Malcolm. In these great, long, rolling epistles, I am really navigating uncharted waters, as it were—and they ask an awful lot of my friends.

I too like the cover on the new issue of *Stars in My Pocket*—though, once again, it's stock art simply slapped on the book. I wonder why, after they paid so much for it, the notion of having an artist actually *paint* a cover for the novel is so anathema to them. Good as that cover is, the book has *still* never had its own.

Yes, I am saddened by the dim news in your arthritis treatment—not a little because I suspect I am headed in the same direction. Started on high blood pressure medicine about three months ago, now—which, of course, is better than *not* starting on high blood pressure medication if you've got high blood pressure. And next letter (after I've been to the urologist's), I'll swap you urinary stories for arthritis tales!

Am still looking for a moment to curl up with the Annual Statistical Report. Why are all things fun the ones we have to put off . . . ?

Here at the university, we have just all sustained an across-the-board four-percent pay cut. For me, that means a drop of about $48.00 a week take home pay—when my combined rent in Amherst and New York City has just risen by some $125.00 a month! (And after a week of two and three degree days, suddenly [it's now February 3rd] we've had a surge of fifty degree weather! Sparrows are chirping outside my office window in the sun . . . !) The one good thing, however, is the suddenly increased quality of the students.

It's a positive note—so I'll end on it: our Associate Head, the same Professor Levine who woke me up to the War, did a large out-of-state mailing last year, pointing out to numerous prospective students that if, in coming to U. Mass., they majored in a field their own state university did not offer, they would get substantial fee reductions here.

It's the law.

So a lot of very bright out-of-state prospective English majors decided, what the hell. My state university has no Comparative Literature Department. Why don't I become a comp. lit. major instead of an English major, and reap the financial benefits . . . ?

For better or worse, out of state students are always brighter than in-state students. And the ones who seem alert enough to take this particular strategy and save themselves some money seem to be just a bit brighter even than that!

The result has been that our department has suddenly gone from having 49 undergraduate majors, as it did three years ago when I got here, to just over 150 undergraduate majors—most of them, by and large, pretty damned smart:

This year my 300-level course, "Introduction to Science Fiction," is packed with the brightest undergraduates I've yet had! Since I began this letter to you, on registration morning, I've had a week of (two) classes with them. Really, at least for me, it's like a different university!

And my graduate seminar, "Science Fiction, Psychoanalysis, and the State," ain't bad either!

Love and stuff
to you, Cynthia, and the boys — cuddles to cats
and bits of good food to the furry ones —

Samuel R. Delany

4

TO KATE SPENCER

March 16, 1991

● ● ●

21 Cowles Lane
Amherst, MA 01002
March 16th, 1991

Dear Kate,

Once again I have to beg your forgiveness for taking so long to write. But it's been a rather fraught couple of months since I received your last letter.

Enclosed is a longish letter I recently wrote to Bob Bravard, that brings you more or less up to date on The Plot. It has a fairly lengthy account of my Uncle Hubert's funeral, back in January. He was eighty-nine. You probably ought to read that one before you read this one. This is basically a continuation of it.

For instance:

A day or two after the funeral, Dennis and I had gone out to breakfast at the Galaxy Deli on Broadway, and there was Jane Anderson, tall and in a rather worn, longish coat, with a scarf around her head. I said hello. "Oh, yes," she said, "mom said she'd seen you at the funeral a couple of days ago!" She was looking for a place to eat, and I told her that the Galaxy was really quite good. "The neighborhood's changed so much in the last couple of years," she said, confidingly.

"Hasn't it!" I said.

Perhaps three more times in the next four days, I bumped into her, coming or going from her old apartment.

Iva's birthday was on the 14th of January. In the letter to Bob, I described Dennis and me taking Iva and her friend Yves out to dinner at Bazzini's in lieu of a celebration.

Ten days later, on January 24th, (my) Dennis turned thirty-seven.

We had a small birthday party for him. Our friends Sam, Leonard,

John Del Gaizo, and Barbara Wise all came—as well as Iva and me. It was lots of fun. (Though I do believe Barbara is just a bit jealous of Dennis . . . oh, bite your tongue! Bite your tongue! But she brought him a very nice shirt for a birthday present.) The only friend from his street days that Dennis would have wanted to invite was a wonderful black guy named Lester—another street person whom I'd known and with whom Dennis had been very close. But, a few months before, Lester (who was seriously asthmatic) had gone into the hospital—and died there of heart failure. He was just about Dennis's age. It was really very sad.

Something Dennis did for Lester that quite moved me: about ten days before Lester died, while he was still in the hospital, Lester started watching soap operas, and got quite into one of them. He and Dennis would talk about it on the phone. Well, one of the actresses in the series lived on 72nd Street where Dennis used to panhandle, and she had occasionally given Dennis money and generally been nice to him.

So Dennis went down, hung out in front of the actress's building, and, when she came out one morning, told her he had a friend in the hospital—another homeless person. Would she perhaps just give Lester a phone call and say hello; it would really cheer him up, as he was a great fan of hers.

Bless her, she did. She and Lester apparently talked for half an hour —as Lester had one of the great street senses of humor of all times. And Lester was bubbling about it on the phone for the next week, whenever Dennis called to see how he was doing. Then, a few days later, we learned that Lester had died.

But the street is not kind to the people who live on her.

In the other letter, I described my lecture at the Library on the night of the 22nd. On the afternoon of the same day, I had lunch with Edward Mitchell-Hutchinson of St. Martin's Press, his boss, Michael [?], head of the St. Martin's college textbook division, and St. Martin's SF editor Gordon Van Gelder. You know Mitchell-Hutchinson's name because he sent you that SF text-book proposal to review. Apparently he was impressed enough with our reviews to (one) reject the book and (two) ask if I would like to put one together for St. Martin's myself. Fundamentally, I've agreed—though I won't really get started working on it till this summer, at the very soonest.

When I do, I may very well be asking you for input!

Dennis and I came back to Amherst. Shortly thereafter, Barbara Wise came up for a three day visit. She stayed at the Lord Jeff Inn, that faces on to the green and sloping stretch of Amherst Commons, with its few, winter-sparse trees. We spent most of her three days here out at the mall seeing two movies a day: I believe we got in *Edward Scissorhands*, *L.A. Story*, *The Grifters*, *Hamlet*, and at least two more, though at this distance their names escape.

At the beginning of February I did a week-long visit to the University of Maine at Orono. It was a nine hour bus trip (including the two hour layover at Boston). On the bus, I met a fascinating, and rather sad, kid —I say kid, but he was thirty. Gary was a carpenter, married, a little guy—half a head shorter than I am—with hair that, in adolescence, had probably been red, though now it was brown with a kind of copper underhue. A very basically handsome face, a muscular body, he nevertheless had pimply skin. He was from Fall River, Massachusetts—and, incidentally, besides being an inveterate nail biter, had the biggest hands I think I've ever seen on a human being! Really, they were close to being deformed. Two weeks ago, he'd broken up with his wife, who was thirty-three and to whom he'd been married for seven years—they had no children. Now the plan was to get back together and spend a weekend at Bar Harbor, where they would talk things out and see if they wanted to patch things up.

He was very anxious for things to work out.

They lived outside a tiny town 50 miles north of Bangor, called Machias. According to him, neither one of them was seeing anyone else. The main problem was simply that she was bored to death—complicated by the fact that he had handled their money poorly—mainly investing it in property when the real estate situation in New England was moving into the disastrous. They owned three houses, presumably worth well over a hundred-fifty-thousand the three of them. But they couldn't sell any of them.

Most of the desire for the break seemed to have come from her. In anticipation of their weekend together, he'd brought her a diamond that he was planning to give her.

At our various stops, he tried to call her—to make sure she would meet him in Bangor, as they'd planned. He'd spoken to her that morning on the phone, and she'd said definitely she'd meet him there with the car. But, he said, she could be real changeable. And at the various stops, when he got off to call, he'd come back, more and more worried because there was no answer at her number. "Man, I hope she ain't changed her mind. I'm really gonna be in trouble, if she decides she don't wanna meet me no more."

He seemed an incredibly good hearted fellow. Indeed, the only fault I could see in his personality was that he had a tendency to talk your ear off—but that might have just been nervousness. Still, if he went on like that to her alone in the wilderness north of Machias, I could see how it might have been a problem for her.

During the course of our hours together, he must have told me most of his life story. I've got pages of notes on him that I jotted down later that evening in my notebook.

They include such things as:

Gary had carpal tunnel surgery on his wrists, when, a few years ago, he found his hands constantly growing numb and that he was dropping glasses of milk and small objects.

As a child in Fall River, he'd come home, tripped over something in the dark hallway, fallen on top of it, pushed himself up, and, frightened, run up the stairs into his apartment—to find his arms covered with blood. Downstairs, a man had been stabbed in the hallway seventeen times and the lights put out. Nine-year-old Gary had fallen over the corpse.

By his own count, twenty-three of Gary's childhood friends are currently dead from violent means—drugs, cars, knifings, shootings.

Gary's older brother, after both his feet were amputated, was diagnosed as having Berenger's disease—an allergic reaction to nicotine. The amputations could have been prevented if he'd have given up smoking.

Though his accent is the bluntest of New England working class (". . . dese, dose, an' dem . . . Gary talked to me for almost five hours without ever using any profanity. The closest he came to "bad language" was, when describing his older brother who had recently had both legs amputated at the knee, he said: "Imagine, not bein' able to get out of the bath tub by your self or take a piss—" at which point his blue eyes beat a moment, as if he might have offended me—"by yourself." And he went on.

At the stop before Bangor, Gary went out to call his wife again. When he came back on the bus, he looked as if someone hit him with a truck. This time, he explained, he'd gotten through. She wasn't going to meet him. She didn't want to see him. There was nothing to talk about. It was over.

He curled up in his side of the seat, went to sleep, and had small, twitching nightmares for the last hour of the ride.

Welch Everman was my host. (I got Welch to drive the somewhat distraught Gary to a motel, when he met me at the bus stop.) In the course of my week at the University, I took over thirteen classes, did a public lecture, gave a public reading, attended a reception and three more or less formal dinners with the faculty. On the last night, the graduate students (many of whom taught the classes I'd taken over), threw me a fine Maine lobster dinner at one of their houses. Then there was the nine hour bus trip back to Amherst.

In late February Dennis and I went down to New York again. I was scheduled to read at the Gay and Lesbian Alliance on West 13th Street on the evening of the 28th. The night we arrived, it was snowing.

We met Iva at the apartment, then walked up to Duke's Steak House on the corner of Columbus Avenue, for dinner. The trees down the block made a white crystal canopy over both sides of the street. The branches looked, I told Iva, ". . . like giant, three dimensional doilies."

"Now that," said my daughter, shrugging her collar up around her neck, "is the last thing I would have compared them to. They're beautiful. But I never would have thought that."

A day later, my sister called to tell me that still another uncle, my late father's last surviving brother, had died. Uncle Hap was 95 and had been blind and in a nursing home for several years. The funeral was much smaller than Uncle Hubert's and was—somewhat surprisingly—not at St. Martin's; rather it was at a small funeral parlor about a block west of where I grew up in Harlem as a child. Indeed, as my sister said, "This is probably a lot more like the funerals dad used to have." The minister was a real old fashioned Harlem preacher, of the sort I haven't heard for quite some time. He was pretty much up there in years, but he was lively. And he had apparently been married by my grandfather, the Bishop, some time back in the twenties, somewhere in North Carolina.

Once again, my father's two surviving sisters, Sadie (shortly to be a hundred-two) and Bessie (a week shy of her hundredth birthday) came to the funeral.

"I was planning," Aunt Bessie said, smiling, as the two of them sat in the lobby of the Harlem funeral parlor on Eighth Avenue and 132nd Street (while Uncle Hap lay in state in the chapel. I only learned during his eulogy that "Hap" was a nickname he'd picked up back in dental school—because he was so happy!), surrounded by friends, nephews, nieces, grandnephews, and grandnieces, "to live to a hundred-twenty. But I really don't think I want to anymore." (Aunt Bessie had been a dentist too; she and Uncle Hap used to share an office on 7th Avenue and 133rd Street when I was a child, although she'd retired when I was three or four; but Hap had filled my teeth half a dozen times.)

"Although," Aunt Sadie added, pensively, "age definitely has its advantages."

Alas, I didn't have a chance to ask her what they were. Approaching 49 in days, and just having started a new and better high blood pressure medication (40 mgs of Corgard in the morning; 5 mgs of Vesotech in the evening), I haven't figured them out yet.

The day Dennis and I took the bus back up here to Amherst, it poured rain.

Here at U. Mass., things have been a mite confused.

During our recent war, a young teacher sat down in the middle of Amherst Commons, soaked himself in paint thinner, and burned himself to death as a war protest—perhaps two-hundred-yards from my front door. His name was Gregory Levine; he was thirty years old and worked as a substitute teacher in Hadley, a nearby little town, and was journalist Ellen (Pulitzer Prize, *Boston Globe*) Goodman's stepson. Because half of Amherst's shops are on two sides of the Commons, everyone who worked there saw it. For the next week, whenever you went in somewhere to buy a stick of gum, a newspaper, or a roll of Scotchtape, it was all anyone behind the counters could talk about.

It happened about 1:53 in the afternoon—when I was home, taking a nap. To make things worse, the previous day a house had burned down around the corner from me, maybe half a dozen homes away. Two undergraduate men had lost their lives. At least one thing that was to blame was that the landlord had not gotten around to installing a smoke detector.

A few hours after the self-immolation, when I was up and about, I ran into one of my students in front of the copy center, who started to talk about the incident.

I had not heard about the fireball on the Commons, however, and thought he was talking about the burning the previous day — and kept making these comments about smoke detectors . . . which, from his odd frowns, I assume he must have thought were unbelievably tasteless jokes on my part! When we parted, we were still talking wholly past each other.

Only an hour later did I hear about it — and only then was I shocked and, indeed, mortified to realize how callous I must have sounded to the young man.

Really, though, the whole town was devastated. There was a constant memorial on the spot where he died, that, in effect, lasted for several days — with people, candles, flowers, night and day. For a week, I was quite depressed. I couldn't even get my thoughts together enough to write about it in my journal.

There was a while there when I was really rather worried about myself. I'd be standing at the stationery counter, and someone would be saying to the young woman selling papers behind the counter — in order to protect themselves from the emotional hurt of the incident (I would realize this clearly): "Well, he's was probably just crazy. I'm sure that's the real reason he did it —"

And I would find myself interrupting: "It doesn't matter whether he was crazy or not. You just can't disqualify an act like that. What we decided was acceptable to do to those people in the bunker yesterday in Iraq, he simply decided was acceptable to do to himself. If it was a mistake — and I think it was — crazy or not, it was a very *little* mistake that he made. You won't make it better by saying he was nuts! You just have to experience it in all its full and very deep tragedy!" Then I would turn around and stalk angrily from the store, to find myself in tears on the street, minutes later, while I passed the stretch of green on which Gregory had soaked himself in two gallons of paint thinner and set himself—with his second match; a passing father with his three-year-old daughter, not having any idea what he was about to do, saw the first he lit go out—on fire, virtually exploding in a ten-foot ball of flame and a column of black smoke, staggering to his feet and burning for perhaps two minutes, while people ran to try and put him out, futilely, with their coats.

Unlike the Vietnamese monks, he apparently did not sedate himself with drugs first.

At any rate I must have said things like that at least five times. I suspect I was becoming quite a pest.

But it was the sixth self-immolation in the country since December—the last one having been on the White House lawn a couple of months back.

I bought all the papers covering it I could, planning to cut out the articles and make a kind of commemorative scrap book. A month later, however, the papers are still in a pile in the corner.

But I'm feeling better about it now.

Last week, indeed, I had a strange day of dizzy spells in class and—after sleeping away the rest of the afternoon—nausea in the evening. But my doctor has changed my blood pressure medication, and I seem to be substantially better.

The University itself is in complete chaos. We've lost six deans in the last month—including mine. The President and the Chancellor of the University have both left for other places. The Board of Regents has just been fired.

And I'm the Acting Head of my department—which means, as some wag pointed out to me the other day, there is nobody in any position of power between me and the Governor!

But we are mucking through.

My classes are going well, however. They're the brightest I've had since I've been teaching here—though my Intro. to SF class is a little bewildered by the notion of "the object" in philosophical terms. I've occasionally spoken of "the tyranny of the subject," but I'm only just beginning to realize how apt a phrase that is, in terms of these kids' ability to think in materialist terms.

But "Science Fiction, Psychoanalysis, and the State" is really doing some exciting work: it's my graduate seminar, and consists of ten young men—we had one woman, but I think she got scared and dropped out. I wish I could say I was sorry, but she had an unbelievably grating personality and insisted on interrupting me every thirty seconds (no exaggeration) and bringing up total irrelevancies. It's sad to have to say it, but we were all relieved when she didn't show up for the second class —nor has she since.

We've had two promotions this year, and in one case I had to write up the scholarship—which involved reading a very good manuscript on Kant and still another on Kierkegaard. But, as you might imagine, it was slow going.

The world is a strange place. A friend of mine just left off in my mailbox a Xerox of a page from a gay paper that cites "The Fifty Most Influential People in Gay & Lesbian Literature in the Past Decade" (The *Lambda Book Report*, which comes out of Washington D.C.): It includes pictures and blurbs of both myself and Marilyn, as well as various friends and acquaintances, such as (the late) Joe Beam, Pat Califia, and Marty Duberman.

Enclosed, for you folks, is a little . . . stuff.

It's getting on to eight o'clock. I'm cooking some fish tonight as soon as I get up from here. Dennis and I (who have been together a year this month) catch an early bus for New York City tomorrow to spend the week of my Spring break with Iva in New York.

Much love to you
and your own wonderful
Dennis—

Samuel R. Delany

PS—Let me obsess over the burning on Amherst Commons just a page or two more. When I was going over the newspaper articles, one incident kept leaping out. Recently opened about six months ago, Nancy James' Restaurant faces the left side of the Commons (if *you* face the Lord Jeff). It's a little breakfast and lunch place, painted blue inside, that sells rather mediocre "home-baked" goods. But someone having lunch there saw the flames — saw other people running across the grass — and ran out of the restaurant to see what was happening. His account made several of the papers. Several of them reported the restaurant's name, however, as "Mary Jane's." In other places, I know, you've read me write about how such fudged facts plague the occasional newspaper accounts of my own doings — from the papers, for example, it would be impossible to tell whether I had a daughter named Iva or a son named Ivan. And there'd been an article in the *Bangor Daily News* (for Sat–Sun. February 9th–19th, by one Dale McGarrigle), about my visit to the university there. McGarrigle had called me at my office in Amherst a couple of days before I'd left and interviewed me by phone. In the course of his interview, he'd asked me how I liked being a professor. I told him, quite clearly: "I find it creating more difficulties than not. I don't have enough time to read and very little time to write." In the article, however (otherwise pretty accurate), this comes out: "I find plenty of time to read [!], but very little time to write." Possibly because of this, back in Amherst, I found myself dwelling on the "Mary Jane's / Nancy James" confusion, sitting on my bed and looking over a handful of the papers that had gotten the name wrong and comparing it to the accounts that had gotten it right. Indeed, there were a number of other discrepancies as well in the quotes from the handful of witnesses: a small statue of Buddha was found "near" the charred body — but was it Levine's? Or had it just been left there by someone else? I found myself dwelling on — really, an extension of the general biographical questions I've been wrestling with for a decade or more now — the impossibility (from the report of the old school friend working in the Hadley paint store who'd sold Levine the paint thinner that morning, to the tenant in Levine's house who used to hear him playing his banjo in his back room, to the recollections of an English professor at the University, my colleague Jules Chemetsky, who'd taught Levine as an undergraduate and had been a friend of his family's) of putting together a "true" account of the what-and-why of that unseasonably mild February afternoon.

At any rate, Dennis likes to sleep late; I tend to rise early.

And a day or so later, at about eight-thirty, when the temperature had gone down again to something more usual for February, muffled in scarf, knitted "New York Bad-Boys" cap, and winter coat, I found myself wandering into Nancy James, sitting down and ordering their breakfast special: cranberry pancakes — with a side of sausage.

I ate my breakfast but, toward the end of my second cup of decaf, found myself growing nauseated. Nancy James's restrooms are down in the basement. It's an old building with very low ceilings. Suddenly I stood up, hurried into the back and loped down the steps — they'd put a big floor-to-ceiling mirror along one basement wall and I saw myself flash by, looking distraught — and just made it into the white-painted booth-sized men's room, where I threw everything up, quite violently, retching and retching, as though the restaurant itself had become a node of confusion, with no fixed identity: and everything in it, including me, had become infected with its lost precision, as if I were suffering from some sort of ontological sea-sickness.

After about five minutes, I rinsed my mouth out, flushed the toilet, came back upstairs, paid, and left the restaurant. I don't think anyone noticed what had happened — or at least no one indicated it. But I couldn't tell you if there was some emotional connection behind and between the articles and all this — or if it were just the onset of a mild, twenty-four-hour stomach flu. While this is perhaps an extremely over-romantic reading, I nevertheless went home feeling grim.

Still, it was that kind of week.

Fortunately it seems to be well over with.

5

TO ERIN MCGRAW

September 24, 1991

· · ·

21 Cowles Lane

Amherst MA 01002

Sept. 24th, 1991

Dear Erin,

Remember, now—you *said* you enjoyed memoirs.

That, at any rate, explains the eccentrically titled book enclosed. Yes, the cover-lad is me, some thirty years and a hundred pounds ago. It's astonishing what changes time chooses to send the body through!

Also, I send on a review of the Lehman book, *Signs of the Times* (plus a review of his poems, *Operation Memory*), from *American Book Review* —though I feel even reviewer Simpson's characterization of the "de Man affair" is unnecessarily sensationalistic:

". . . a distinguished Yale professor of comparative literature and a leading light in the dissemination of American deconstruction was discovered to have written pro-Nazi Op-ed pieces for the Belgian national daily between 1940 and 1942." Come on; the pieces were book reviews, for heaven's sakes; not Op-ed pieces by any stretch—though they sometimes appeared across from the editorial page. And the anti-Semitic material (not pro-Nazi material: there is a difference) was restricted to three points made in passing, confined to three paragraphs, in two articles—out of 104 that the precocious de Man wrote for the paper between ages 19 and 21!

In general, however, I pretty much endorse what Simpson has to say about the book proper.

And he is more measured than I, certainly.

It seems to me strange, Erin, to give an account of an intellectual movement; but, to make that account recognizable to the people who consider themselves within it, you have to insert a "not" before the verbs in more than half the sentences!

But that's how Lehman's account of deconstruction struck me, at any rate.

Look—I'll send you Xeroxes of two essays by de Man. "Criticism and Crisis" is the opening of his first important book, *Blindness and Insight* (1971). "Semiology and Rhetoric" is the opening of his second major offering (all he really lived to complete in a form he oversaw through publication), *Allegories of Reading* (1979). Both are widely informed, passionate, and polemical. You read them—and *you* decide if you are being snared in the coils of a crypto-Nazi contaminated with racism and anti-Semitism.

As Simpson says, you'll learn a lot more about de Man that way than you will from David Lehman.

Erin, I do think that American intellectuals, in general, are terrified of thinking. I don't mean to say that we're lazy. On the contrary, we often outwork our European contemporaries in sheer, Germanic, intellectual labor. Still, it seems to me that many of us suspect that if we are caught at it, we will lose all our connections with that group that we will not even go so far as to characterize as "the masses," or "the common man or woman," because to characterize them—even to suggest that the group has characteristics—is to broach criticizing people who wish to remain a silent majority, an invisible majority, a majority who can respond terroristically to anything perceived as articulation, much less criticism.

I read *Poets in Their Youth* when it first came out, and enjoyed it muchly. I don't remember—did the bears come from Delmore Schwartz's "The Heavy Bear That Goes with Me"? That image delighted me as a high school reader of Oscar Williams' anthologies; it even emerges, ghost-like, in "They Fly at Çiron."

Speaking of which:

The short story collection (title: *Driftglass/Starshards*, and it contained a copy of Çiron) got off to Malcolm Edwards at Grafton Books, to the tune of $42.00 overseas express postage (Whew!) on the morning of September 9th.

I kept fiddling with "They Fly at Çiron," however, even after I sent the stories over. "One does not finish a work of art. One abandons it," said wise Valéry. So finally, I decided that, even if it wasn't finished, it was near time to jump ship.

My friend Don Levine (another Comp. Lit. professor, he) came over on Thursday afternoon at about four, and spent till ten-thirty reading it over, making suggestions. (He's a good reader; and the majority of his suggestions were right on.) Then he, Dennis (my very significant other), and I all went out to a rather exhausted dinner at our impoverished little town's impoverished little notion of a Good Little Restaurant: Judy's — where everything tastes the same. (But the seafood bisque is decent.) Then I came home and spent till two in the morning implementing Don's suggestions.

As the early hours rolled over in the darkness outside my study windows, I added a death bed scene, took out words (always take out words, words, words), pumiced and polished and rouged to a deep shine. Next morning I added still another scene — then immediately took it out and turned it into an appendix.

When short stories get appendices, we must acknowledge they've jumped genre. Yes, this is all going somewhere, but —

Another adventure intrudes here: the BBC had commissioned an independent production TV crew, Moonlight Films, to come to the States and make a documentary on Black Science Fiction in the U.S. Black Science Fiction in the U.S. is basically Octavia E. Butler (the "E" stands for Estelle), Steven Barnes, and me. There are also perhaps half a dozen black artists working in the overground comic book industry today — and the producer had had what I'm sure he'd thought was a wholly original notion, of expanding the topic to cover what these artists were up to: some real visuals. (I've been writing about the intimate relation of comic books and American SF for twenty years now. But . . .) The crew was filming in New York that weekend and had asked me to come down and take part.

About two weeks before I'd said, "Yes."

So, after my Thursday night marathon on Çiron, on Friday morning at eleven, I leapt from the word processor and the last Çiron work (which I'd started in on about 8:30 a.m.), dove into and out of the shower (psychic blood a-gush from the wounds of separation, while I explained to my wet self, under the rufflings of the big, navy Ikea towel, this is going to be *good* for you, good for the story; it'll give you *distance* . . .), threw some stuff in an oblong overnight bag, and sprinted up North Pleasant Street to the Peter Pan bus stop; at five past noon I hopped on the green and white bus and rode on down—for four-and-a-half hours—to New York, while, on my Walkman, I listened to one side of Harry Chapin's *Short Stories*, followed by all three cassettes of Yo-Yo Ma playing Bach's first six suites for unaccompanied cello.

Like the kids say: awesome!

At Hartford, we were joined by an Hispanic group who sprawled among the back seats and sang what I assumed to be Cuban gospel music, now in consonance, now in dissonance, with the cello.

[Says my Journal, written just after I got home:]

Finally I moved on to Nilsson (*Schmilsson*). As we were coming down Fifth Avenue, to Mt. Morris Park, Nilsson was singing, "I Guess the Lord Must be in New York City." We continued on beside tree-shaded Central park, past the Brisbane monument, that I have been marveling at since childhood.

For the last hour, the light through the bus windows had more and more yellow and red in it, bronzing both the green wall of trees outside the city and the brick and dirt urban confusion within. We got in to Port Authority at about 4:40—and we'd left at noon, making no stops on the Hartford/NYC leg at all.

[From still another entry, recalling it all, The Journal goes on to say:]

Tues, Sept. 17, 1991: Last Friday, when I got down to New York, I had a bumpy and thumpy 4:30 cab ride (through the thick four-thirty traffic) from Port Authority up to 82nd Street, with a cabby (a middle-aged Pakistani) who, from the odd near-accident we had down below 59th and the violence of his curses when other cabbies cut him off on the dusty, sunny Avenue, I decided was half mad.

Lugged my briefcase and the Cardin overnight up my five flights, and shouldered inside—a bit more exhausted than usual with my progressive arthritis and the general exhaustion of the day.

The paint along the ceiling of the hall still hangs in shreds and water stained filaments (making Marilyn, when she comes, say—not appreciatively—the apartment looks like a crack-den; at least in the hall).

Iva wasn't home.

I put my stuff down on the red rug in the living room.

Iva had told me on the phone the previous night that she had a rid-ing lesson at four, and it was just around five, so I decided—after I got my breath back—to walk up toward the Claremont Stable. If her lesson wasn't over yet, I'd meet her either there or on the way home. So, on my knees' wobbling wrecks, it was down the five flights again, across, around, and up Amsterdam.

The stable is on 89th Street, but I'd only got two blocks (glancing up at the street signs all too frequently), when I looked down. Three quarters of a block ahead of me, Iva was coming along, in her riding pants.

With his bowl of curly hair belling to his shoulders, boyfriend Chris was on her left. Black hair a-frizz all around and a head shorter than them both, another girl was on her right.

Iva saw me—waved, called: "Hi, Dad!"

Two blocks, and five flights later, we were all up in the living room again. (Iva: "Dad, mom says your apartment looks like a crack Den." Yes, yes—I know.) The other little girl was Rebecca—friend of Chris's, whom Iva had mentioned to me last phone conversation.

Yes, I had brought down the cowboy boots (given to me by tall, red-headed Dr. Felberbaum) for Chris, who tried them on in the living room. They seemed to fit.

Chris and Rebecca left. Iva and I went out to dinner at Bazzini's, up on Columbus Avenue, where maitre d' and owner, Max, pulled up a stool, sat beside our booth, and regaled us with tales of potato cro-quettes, spaghetti (your choice), and how badly the restaurant seems to be doing.

Back at home, I was going on about how disorganized the TV peo-ple from England seemed—there was only one message on the box (small, black plastic, with one blinking red light, on the floor between the manuscript-mounded coffee table's foot and the maroon, modular chair) from Moonlight's liaison person, Paul Coleman, saying they were leaving Los Angeles within hours and would be in New York shortly. But it included neither time nor date. Nor did it give any number where I could reach them. Have they been here for two days? Are they *en route*? So far (I explained to Iva, now that it was 10:30 p.m.), all I was going on was a telephone conversation which said they would like to film me on Saturday afternoon, after they finished shooting some visuals at Marvel Comics. Really, it was only on the strength of about three such phone calls that I'd come down. Not one letter had gone back (or forth)—

Phone rang.

It was Paul.

Moonlight was in New York. But they'd had to change hotels. Could they get me tomorrow morning?

Sure. Would they be coming here?

No. Could I come there?

Certainly. Would it be possible to bring my daughter along, who wanted to watch a couple of hours of the filming, before she went off to a driving lesson.

Absolutely. They'd call about eight-thirty tomorrow and tell me exactly when to come down.

Next morning at seven-thirty, I was up, showered—shampooed my beard, then filled it full of Iva's mousse and hair spray. It was rather like having a piece of shapely Styrofoam glued to my face. But, given my previous experience with filming, I was sure it was a good idea.

At nine-thirty, Paul called.

Could I be down at the Mayflower Hotel, on 63rd and Central Park West in twenty minutes?

What about an hour, said I, to allow me to get some breakfast? You *had* said afternoon . . .

On the other end of the phone, Paul made an unhappy sound—

All right, I said. Twenty minutes.

The director wants to shoot you on top of a sky scraper.

I believe I mentioned to you the last time you brought this up, said I, that I suffer from severe acrophobia. I can't go anywhere near a railing or anything like that—

Don't worry, said a worried Paul. We'll take care of it.

So Iva and I, with an umbrella and a plastic bag containing brush, more hair spray, and a small towel, went down, got a cab, and zipped off to the Mayflower—or, rather tried to zip. Seems there was a Crafts Festival on Columbus Avenue that day, so that all traffic was being diverted, etc.

Three blocks away from the hotel, to avoid still another tie-up, we got out and walked the rest of the way.

It was a gray-green day, overcast, with a definite threat of rain.

Central Park billowed greenly above its black stone wall. And the glass doors of the Mayflower reflected the trees across from it behind gilded "M"s.

In the lobby, in white jeans and a black t-shirt, a young, slight (East) Indian sat, who looked up at me with that familiar-questioning of stranger looking out for stranger.

"Hello," I said, stepping in with a smile. "You must be Paul Coleman. I'm Chip Delany. This is my daughter Iva . . ."

Paul invited Iva and me in to the Mayflower Restaurant, while I mentioned they'd chosen *the* hotel in the city where everyone connected with TV and video always stayed.

Yes, Paul said, that had begun to come clear to them—after they'd been there for a couple of hours. But, really, their moving to the Mayflower had been an accident. They hadn't known its previous reputation.

In the hotel restaurant, we got a gesture at breakfast. I had coffee, juice, and an English muffin; Iva had juice, an English muffin and a side order of bacon—which we ended up sharing. And while we ate, Paul told me their tale of woe. First: The camera man—a six-foot-eight Englishman named John—had broken his ankle, filming somewhere out on the rocks of some Los Angeles beach. Moments after we got the story, the gentleman in question—all nose and teeth and stringy hair —limped in to say something . . . on a towering crutch that would probably have done nicely for somebody six-foot-four, but which was clearly too short by a head for this scruffy crane of a thirty-five-year-old!

But it had been the largest one they'd had at the Los Angeles hospital where he'd been treated . . .

Also, apparently, the comic book artists they'd been supposed to film that morning had not been as flexible (read: cooperative) as I was—so they were going to have to get them later. (One of their horror stories was that, when they'd gotten off the plane in Los Angeles, an entire case full of lenses was simply missing! Then the camera man had broken his ankle. Paul shook his head: "I don't think I've ever been on a shoot before that's been plagued with such bad luck.") Out in L.A., Butler had been easy to work with. Barnes had been difficult to film, however, "because he insisted on spending all his time joking and clowning around with the technical crew—and although it was very funny, he wouldn't let us get anything done." This apparently explained why I was being kept down in the restaurant until they were actually ready to film— in case I turned out to be another clown. The director—whom I still hadn't met—was named Terence or Derek or some such . . . I never did get it straight. Now and again, various men and women in jeans, with little pouches about their waists and clipboards on their arms—Susan, Karen, John, Keith—would drop in to the restaurant from upstairs, with reports to Paul, who was going to do the actual interviewing with me.

John (not cameraman John, but lighting John), a normally tall (six-one, six-two) blond, bushy-headed Englishmen, had actually read a number of my novels, and seemed very pleased to meet me. (Turned out we also shared some film enthusiasms, including Kathryn Bigelow and Sam Peckinpah.) But I'd begun to suspect that Paul had looked at no more than a few pages of any of my books. The questions he told me he was going to ask were, all of them, simply sentences I'd said to him three weeks before in a trans-Atlantic conversation, re-formed into interrogatives. I wondered if I was not supposed to recognize them.

Around eleven, when Paul went off upstairs, Iva (who is a poised and lovely creature), confessed she was bored to tears. (It's hard for kids to watch their parents made much of, especially when it happens slowly— and, at that hour-and-a-half hotel breakfast, not much had happened.) Would I mind if she went?

Not at all, I told her. Have a good driving lesson at one.

Ten minutes later, Paul returned. They were ready for me upstairs. The hotel had given us a room to work in, he explained. We rode up on an elevator of mirrors and brass and lush carpeting—but then, it was a kissin' cousin to the one in the hotel you and I were lodged in at the Imagination Conference. So you know it.

The room the hotel had given us to film in was really quite sumptuous—in a very different way from the suites we got in Cleveland.

The Mayflower is a rather old building; thus, its modernity ends with the lobby, halls, and elevators. The actual rooms are old fashioned. This room—on the twenty-first floor—was full of floor to ceiling book shelves . . . with *books* in them—more than unusual in a hotel! Alas, none of this was to be filmed. The room also had two balconies—one of which was a full terrace, with garden furniture sitting out on it.

Unfortunately, everything was aimed in the other direction. In deference to my acrophobia, they'd set up a chair in front of the double-doors of glass, leading up some wooden steps out to the smaller balcony, across which you could see some of the park and a smidge of New York skyline.

The chair was balanced with one leg on a reticulated aluminum equipment case; some books were under the other leg; and the back legs were on the steps—the most unsteady looking of seats!

Meanwhile, a pleasant Brit in jeans and a white t-shirt, Karen ("Are you the recordist?" "Yes, that's me!") scotch taped a pea-sized microphone to the inside of my shirt, and put a broadcaster in the inside pocket of my own aqua t-shirt (that I wore beneath the black plaid over shirt). Then, settling back on the couch beside me, she delved into the padded case, strapped to her shoulder, to tune and retune the dials and nobs of her Nagra.

[Yet another Journal entry, written at the time, in the room as I sat on the couch, waiting for the setting up to be completed:]

The guys set up lights, move the camera, adjust the chair before the window—while it verges on a drizzle outside. The Mayflower hotel has given the Moonlight crew a rather sumptuous, if long and narrow, room, with balconies at both ends.

Chatting now with Coleman—

This entry got interrupted by a conversation with blond and bespectacled production assistant, Susan, who, it turns out, some years before, had been an exchange student from England at U. Mass, like my little wonder student of three years ago, Boyd Hilton.

As blue gels and wax-papery light dispersers went up over the big, indoor spotlight, Susan explained that they needed another cameraman. Did I have any ideas?

In the suite's bedroom (with canopied bed!), I gave her two names, Gerry Fyle (husband of old elementary school friend, Hyla, whom I still sometimes see, and who'd been cameraman on [the old film version of] *Lord of the Flies*) and Jack Newman (cameraman on my ex-lover Frank

Romeo's two films, *Bye-bye Love* and *The Aunts*). I wasn't very sanguine about either, since the Fyles always summer on the Cape; and, last time I'd seen him, five/six years ago, Jack had been making serious "must-move-to-L.A.-and-make-some-real-money" noises. But it was the best I could do, off the top of my head.

Though broke-foot John could handle the sedentary interviewing, for the next day's mobile work, they needed a camera who could get around, Susan explained.

"Good luck," I said, as she went off to try them.

And I went back to the living room.

"Put a spot out on the balcony there, to throw something on him from the left," John directed, sitting on a chair, his ghastly foot, much too swollen for a shoe or a sock, up on another aluminum box. The swelling went down to the toes and well up above the ankle. And there was a bad sore at one place, so that—he had told me earlier—not only was he afraid it was broken, but that there was an internal infection. Given that it had happened three days ago, it looked like it.

At the back table, our little blond gorilla of an assistant cameraman, Dave (an American), was up to his elbows in the black bag, loading film.

Now the director came over to speak with me for about five pleasant minutes. In a blue designer shirt, blue slacks, and blue running shoes, he was a slender, good looking black guy of about thirty-five, with an educated English accent. He had the air of a quietly worried man whose job, right now, said that he ought to be relaxed, cheerful, and comfortable.

We chatted about five minutes—about nothing to do with the show at all.

My take on him from that time—though I might be wholly wrong —was that he was a young guy who'd worked in commercial design (probably advertising), doing still photography, at which he might well have been quite good. He'd always wanted to do films, but now that he was behind the camera, he'd found that he really didn't have much of a handle on things that moved . . .

For the last three minutes, we did talk about the show:

"What do you think we should do after the interview?"

"Huh?" I said. This is not the sort of question one expects to get from the director—if one is a performer.

"I'd read somewhere that the Brooklyn Bridge was very important to you . . . I thought, perhaps, we'd go down there and get a couple of shots of you walking on it . . . ?"

The only place he could have read that was on the blurb on the back of the paperback edition of my autobiography.

"Now that's an interesting idea," I said, deciding that the man was really something of a dolt.

"We'd like to get you reading a few short passages from your work, too, of course . . ."

"You really should have told me," I said. "I would have brought something —"

"We have a book of yours downstairs — *Dhalgren*?"

"Well, all right. It's coming out in England in a few months for the first time. And your show's scheduled for the end of November. That might not be a bad idea." I breathed an internal sigh of relief. (I mean, they might have had nothing for me to read from but *The American Shore*!) "You know," I said, thinking fast, "the book takes place in a burned-out urban landscape, inspired by burned-out-central Harlem, here in the city — the sort Harlem has become since the 1960s. It might be interesting to have me reading from the book against some dilapidated building up there — that's where I grew up, you know."

Terence or Derek brightened. "Sounds wonderful," he said. (I had been just about to say, But you would have had to scout out locations when you were here last month . . .) "That's what we'll do, then. Keith, do you want to run down to my room and get that copy of Mr. Delany's *Dhalgren* . . . ?"

Even without getting to Steve Barnes's clownishness, Keith and I were, by now, on a first name basis. But what the hey. Keith ran off.

"We'll drive up after lunch!"

(I cannot imagine, at union rates, working with a crew of ten this way.)

Three minutes later, when Keith was back, he left me to find a suitable passage in the book.

Paul drifted back.

And minutes later I was up on the chair; lights were on, film was rolling . . .

Although I get interviewed regularly, and get asked the same questions again and again, I can never remember individual questions from individual sessions—even minutes after it's over. When, after I've come from an interview, lovers or relatives or friends ask: "What did they *ask* about? What did they want to *know*? What did *you* say?" I draw a blank.

What I recall is the general emotional feel of the interview session. And in this case, for the first forty minutes of it, the feeling was dull, competent, and low-key. In the course of forty minutes of film (with ten or fifteen minutes between each ten minute canister), they didn't change the position of the camera, once!

Nor were there any covering shots. It was all single-shot, full-face, dead-on close up—with the faintest suggestion of New York skyline in the background.

For the last ten minutes of film, however, the director took Paul into the back of the room and conferred with him. Then, when we started again—same angle, same close up—the questions were a lot more pointed.

My answers were a lot more impassioned—and I found myself thinking, this is what should have been going on for the *last* couple of hours, now!

Then, it was two-thirty; we were to break for lunch, before the location shots.

By this time I'd decided that the mousse and the hair spray had been a pretty good idea. (We ended up filming from just before noon till past ten-thirty at night.) Paul, me, and three or four of the crew were sent around the corner to a deli for sandwiches.

Down in the lobby, Paul and I tried to round up sandwich orders. Then, with Keith, Karen (the recordist), and (lighting) John, we took off down 63rd Street, crossed a fantastically busy Broadway, and went into a huge gourmet food shop that I'd certainly never seen before in my more than forty years in this burg. We proceeded to order our various hams and turkeys and provolones and pasta-pesto salads. (Karen—with that crew-short hair and t-shirt, I want to write "of course"; but that just betrays my last three years among the happy, bouncy, New Age dykes of Northampton—was a vegetarian.) Back at the rather sizable van, I sat inside on the front seat, guarding the food, and Keith (now driver) sat down on the running board, eating a sandwich.

"You know," he said, turning back the wax paper from his ham and cheese, "I don't get the feeling that these people have a very clear idea what they're doing."

The others had all gone back in, to get this, the other, or something else. We — two Americans alone among a bunch of very breezy Brits — I guess had struck up a bond.

"That's kind of my feeling," I said. "I've worked on a couple of films before, and this has the feel of a pretty disorganized shoot."

Keith nodded — and bit. "Now they want to go up to Harlem and take some locations. If what you're looking for is burned out buildings and slums, Harlem's pretty picturesque. But you have to scout things out, plan out what you're gonna do. We'll get something. But we're not gonna get a whole lot, like this."

"*Mmm*," I said, in agreement.

"I just came off a shoot," Keith went on, examining a pickle spear, "where we spent six weeks and three-hundred-thousand dollars getting thirty seconds of film for a commercial. Things get pretty surreal on a shoot like that. But this . . ." He looked up at the beige brick of the May-flower, then shook his head.

With her Nagra over her shoulder, her booms under her arm, and case of tapes and microphones in the other hand, Karen was the first one out of the hotel. "So, we're going up to Harlem, to have you read!" she said, brightly, climbing in. I took the case for her and slid it across between the seats.

They got points, I supposed, in that no one had yet asked me, "Is it dangerous up there?"

"Did you get all the writers reading from their work?" I asked her.

"We got Barnes," she said. "But not Butler."

"Oh, dear," I said. "Why not?"

"Because," Karen said, looking at me as though I ought to know, "she can't read. She's dyslexic."

Now it was my turn to look surprised. "Well, I'm dyslexic, too — " Then I laughed — "but I manage." At which point I decided I'd better drop it.

Though I must tell you a couple of side tales to explain why.

Octavia was my writing student in 1972 at the Clarion SF Writers' workshop. Although, indeed, she was a rather shy young woman of twenty-three, she had no problem reading out her exercises in class. And in 1986, she'd been brought to New York City by the Schomburg Collection of African-American Literature[12] — a division of the New York Public Library — where, one wonderful Saturday afternoon, she and I gave a joint reading to a marvelously appreciative audience, first her, then I. Indeed, now at thirty-seven (as she was in '86), she had been one of the most marvelous poised and presenced women I've ever seen behind a microphone.

But she is a child of L.A., and certainly as film-wise as I was, if not more so. I had a sudden picture of what had struck me about the Moonlight crew as lovably disorganized striking Octavia as rankly incompetent — so that after the interview, she simply threw up her hands and, when they wanted to take her off to find some "meaningful background" against which she might read, she'd simply said: "I'm sorry. I can't read — dyslexic you know," or some such.

"We got some wonderful shots of her on the cliffs above the ocean, north of L.A. She's such an isolated person, you know. She doesn't see very many people. It seemed like a landscape that spoke very much to the person she was."

Octavia lives with her mother — and is about as isolated as any other full-time writer who has to support herself by her work is likely to be. Full-time writing is not a gregarious occupation.

"That's where John broke his foot," Karen concluded, settling into the seat behind me.

Paul came out now.

Then the director.

Then squat, bull-shouldered assistant-cameraman Dave . . .

And (lighting) John and (production assistant) Susan . . .

As they piled in, it got explained: we were leaving (cameraman) John at the hotel because of his foot. Dave would do the location work. Where did I (!?) think we ought to look first . . . ?

12. The Schomburg Center for Research in Black Culture.

Let's try Seventh Avenue—no, Frederick Douglass Boulevard. Yes, that was our best bet . . .

So that's what we did.

Indeed, we passed half a dozen astonishing demolition sites. But it was clear the problem was going to be getting close enough to them to film them as workable backgrounds.

We got a couple of tracking shots (with Dave virtually hanging out the open door of the van, riding along beside me) that followed me walking up Eighth Avenue and turning the corner at 134th Street. From the several groups of black, teen-aged boys hanging out on the street, we got the total range of possible reactions:

From one who dogged us, calling out, "I wan' be in this film! That's okay, now—I'm gon' be in this film, too? Right, man? What you won' me to do? I can dance, sing? You tell me!" to another who, as the camera swept by, quickly pulled his orange t-shirt up over his face and turned away toward the barber shop window, in shoulder-shaking giggles, where some of the patrons were looking out.

Though I'd started off thinking of this as a black production—since it had a black director, an Indian interviewer, and a black star (Ahem . . . me)—suddenly we were all, I think, very aware that the rest of the crew (the majority of people in the van) were white.

We got some shots of me walking up a more residential Harlem street, where a woman, who was overseeing the repaving of a concrete strip in front of her somewhat decrepit brownstone, came up to ask some firm and righteous questions:

"We're doing a documentary about a very fine writer—Samuel R. Delany?—who used to live right around the corner, there," explained Karen, pushing back one earphone of her Nagra. "We're going to show him, revisiting his old neighborhood . . ."

The woman was pleased and, apparently, pacified.

I pointed out to the crew the front of St. Philip's Church at the end of the block, where I'd been an altar boy as a child and had sung for a season in the choir—and had my own not terribly intellectually satisfying theological run-in at 13 (*Motion* §5.2). The old rectory that had housed the Sunday School I'd attended as a child had long since been pulled down; a brick and glass and aluminum community center, itself, after fifteen years looking pretty down at the heels, had replaced it.

In the van once more, we rolled back down Seventh Avenue. I no-ticed—but did not mention—the site of Louis's shoe-shine parlor, just a shadow on the brick wall. I pointed out my own former house—once my father's funeral parlor, now an emergency medical clinic, its sign today in both English and Arabic.

The van door was still open. As we came down below the St. Nicholas Houses, Dave was leaning out, taking some cover footage. We slowed as we passed a black social club, where a good looking young man in green camouflage fatigues sat on a chair below a sign in Arabic that had a pic-ture of Farrakhan on one side and a picture of Malcolm on the other. Some other young men stood at an open door.

As we passed, the seated guy saw us, frowned, and suddenly stood. "Hey!" He stepped toward the curb, in his black turtle neck and green beret. "There better not be no film in that camera—or I'm gonna break it over yo' fuckin' head an' wrap it 'round yo' fuckin' neck!"

Said I, out the door, with my biggest smile: "We're just practicing for an NYU film school class project. It isn't loaded."

"Yeah," said Dave, with fine New Yorker nonchalance. "Don't worry."

And of course, as we were speaking, the van came to a dead halt, just then, in a solid clot of Seventh Avenue four-o'clock traffic.

"Well, okay . . ." said the guy, from the edge of the sidewalk. "But if I see anything on the God damned six o'clock news . . ."

And we sat there smiling at him, him frowning at us, for another, very long, fifty-five seconds, Dave with the camera in his lap now, until the light changed, and the traffic—very, very slowly—eased . . . forward . . . again.

I looked back inside the van; but, bent over their clipboards and deep in conference in the shadowed interior, Paul, Karen, and the director seemed to have totally missed the whole exchange.

Two blocks later, sunlight flaring off the hoods of the river of cars flowing up and down Seventh, in front of the Hotel Teresa (where, so fa-mously, Fidel Castro stayed in New York, so many eons ago), turned our director on. ("No, no—we just have to get this!" He seemed surprised

Harlem had any people in it at all!) We pulled around on 125th and parked, just up in front of a busy bus stop.

"I just want to get a bit of this. You've been working very hard, Chip. You can stay here, if you like."

Which left Keith and me alone again, while the crew went off into the crowds.

Outside the van door, an obese, blind, black kid about eighteen, in a gray shirt and baggy jeans, sat on the sidewalk, his back against the wall, waving his cap and begging, loudly. At the curb, just beside us, there was an impromptu stand selling African pendants and hair bands and American flags and . . . Between them black people hurried up and down the street by the hundreds, fundamentally oblivious to both.

After about fifteen minutes, I told Keith: "I'm just going to run over there, on the off chance they need me—if they don't, I'll be back. You want me to close this door?"

"No," said an equally nonchalant Keith. "Don't bother."

So I got down and walked up toward the Avenue.

"Ah, there you are, Chip. I was just going to send Susan back for you. Do you think you could just walk, from that corner there, over to . . ."

And I was back at work.

We did two or three takes each of at least three shots of me walking through the crowds at 125th Street—one with the Apollo Theater's marquee visible in the background. Till now, despite the make-shift nature of his interview questions, I'd been impressed with Paul's general intelligence. (Perhaps he just hadn't had time to do the sort of research the job actually needed. He wasn't a science fiction fan, and probably had very little real interest in it, anyway.) But 125th Street at 4:30 on a Saturday afternoon is a very crowded place. Literally, thousands of people are crossing the broad Avenue every five minutes. And to set your camera up in the middle of them and film requires some common sense. "Look, guys," I said. "If anyone stops you and asks what you're doing, say that this is a class project for NYU Film School. Everyone in New York has run into NYU film students filming, somewhere or other."

"Oh, no," Paul said (who'd wholly missed our encounter two blocks north), as we stood on the narrow island at the middle of Seventh Avenue, people streaming about us as we set up, "I think it's nice to tell people what the project actually is."

Dave looked at me; I looked at him. We shrugged, and I dashed off to follow the director's instructions. ("The last shot, I was walking camera left to camera right—this one, you've got me going the other way. Do you want my notebook in the same hand? It was in the hand away from the camera, last shot. It'll be in the near hand, this shot—unless you want me to switch it . . . ?")

And when I got back from my various street crossings that were being filmed, Paul was in the center of a bunch of rather loud, black adolescent girls (and one tall, bony boy of fifteen or so, in a huge t-shirt, down to his knees, moonwalking about in front of the camera for all he was worth: "You gettin' this now? You gettin' this?"), ranging from about eight to fifteen, trying to explain, over their gibes, what we were doing.

We loaded up and went back to the van, where Keith fell again to the wheel, as John vaulted in through the back and pulled the door closed.

Now the thing was to find some ruined buildings. At this point, our intrepid assistant cameraman said: "I was just up here, filming three days ago. I can show you a wonderful place with a back alley, and some half fallen down walls . . . Just drive till you see a neighborhood mural, on a wall to your left . . . We'll get out there, and I'll take you right to it."

The place he showed us, though I certainly thought it was picturesque enough, didn't quite grab the director. But, two minutes later, he was out again and across the street.

Across 128th, we found an amazing structure. Through a gate, where some men were working, we went around among the weeds of what had once been an urban back yard and came up on a series of masonry arches, rising above mountains of fallen brick. Slabs of charred beams crossed this way and that among them, against dangling electric cables and water pipes inside three stories of wrecked tenement, one wall and most of the floors fallen away. An absolutely spectacular charred ice-box stood, askew, gaping open near the top of still another hill of bricks—by this time, the light had gone golden in the few minutes before sunset.

In just his sneakers and pants—no shirt—a little gnome of a black guy worked away there furiously, hammering the mortar off the bricks, to resell them. His muscles were like metal bands around his shoulders and back. He was filmed over with gray-white dust, from tightly curled hair to clubbed fingertips, making him look like one of the last of Riefenstahl's Nuba.

The director slipped him a twenty to give us fifteen minutes' quiet—and, at one point, he was supposed to be at the side of one of the shots. But I don't know whether that ever actually happened or not.

At the director's orders, perched at the top of the brick, with Dave pointing his camera up just below me, Karen holding her foot-long, gray, velvety poof of a boom down under the rather worn paperback, and John in the background with a handheld spot blazing over my shoulder, in one of the brick arches, in my most stentorian tones, I read out the *Dhalgren* passage I'd picked:

"Very few suspect the existence of this city. It is as if not only the media but the laws of perception themselves have redesigned knowledge and perception to pass it by. Rumor says there is practically no power here. Neither television cameras nor on the spot broadcasts function: that such a catastrophe as this should be opaque, and therefore dull, to the electric nation! It is a city of inner discordances and retinal distortions . . . A truck had overturned at the block's end. Nearer, three cars, windows rimmed with smashed glass, squatted on skewed hubs, like frogs gone marvelously blind. . . ."

Readings are often tired and tiring things. More times than not, I abhor them—especially my own. But, in the midst of the dozen that, really, are only variant disaster forms, sometimes everything goes right, instead of wrong.

Though most of the rightness, in that case, was the cavernous and catastrophic ambiance of the place, as I finished the first sentence, the entire crew, scattered about at the base of the brick hill, drew in their breaths. And when I'd reached the end, and the director said cut, both he and the recordist, burst out: "Wow!"

We did it a few more times, for full-figure shots—then, at another position; with pipes and burned two-by-sixes a-glitter with charcoal forming equally impressive backdrops.

What was most discouraging about the probable outcome of the Moonlight shoot was, however, most in evidence here. The director would take me by the hand, lead me over drumlins of crumbling brick, and finally position me between two dramatic, ragged walls, a charred beam a-slant between them. Standing a bit below me on the rubble, he'd look up at me against it all, and, with thumbs together so his fingers created the bottom part of an imaginary screen, he'd move his hands around, outlining a shot:

"Okay, now. I think . . . we'll pan down here, pulling back—and catch your face at the bottom, in a tight close up. You'll start to read. Yes, that's it . . ." (Though pulling focus would be tricky, it's a perfectly fine idea for a shot.) Then he'd stagger off on the unsteady footing, calling for camera, lights, and sound.

Each, of course—Dave, John, or Karen—would have to consult with him for two to ten minutes, about technical problems of his or her own. (They were using an electronic slate that wasn't working properly; it kept having to be jiggled and jarred and pounded on the back to get the red numbers on its LED timer to turn over.) Finally, when Dave was at last set up, and actually taking the shot, I'd notice that both the pan and the pull-back had disappeared—no one was pulling focus. And it was clear that it was not because the shot was too difficult, but because, in the flood of technicalities, Terence/Derek had simply forgotten what the original conception of the shot had been.

What he'd have, of course, was another tight or medium close-up of my face, with little or no background to speak of—though, over the most precipitous fallen brick, he had brought us in among the most visually sumptuous ruins to take it. This happened not once, but a good half dozen times—each shot requiring fifteen minutes to a half-an-hour to get.

When you direct, you have to juggle so many factors in each take that to do any creative thinking on the set is nigh impossible. And, if you *do* create there, at the very least you must jot your ideas down. If not, memory alone will defeat you. Also, *shots* are not what a film—even a documentary film—is about. The name of the game is *sequences of shots*. Again, if you arrive at a location and take ten minutes to come up with a sequence, you'd better write it down:

1 (Medium Shot): Chip walks up to gate. (4 Sec's.)
2 (Close Up): Chip's hand opens the gate catch and pulls gate open. (2 Sec's.)
3 (Far Shot): From deep inside the weedy yard, we watch Chip finish opening the gate, come through, and walk toward the camera. (6 Sec's.)
4 (MS tracking): Chip's feet and lower legs walk through weeds, over fallen board, and broken brick. (6 Sec's.)
5 (FS): Pan down the ruined buildings and arches, down the ragged walls and mounds of bricks, to catch Chip, at the bottom, walking away from camera through the weeds to the base of the brick mound. Chip starts to climb the brick. (8 Sec's.)
6 (MS from top of brick mound, looking down): Toward the camera, Chip climbs up the bricks. (4 Sec's.)
7 (MS): Chip steps to the top of the mound, turns, and sits on the ledge of the ruined window arch. From behind him, he takes up a book. (6 Sec's.)
8 (CU): Chip looks down toward the book — which is out of frame. (3 Sec's.)
9 (CU): Chip's hands open the book and he thoughtfully fingers open a few pages. (3 Sec's.)
10 (CU [Continue from 8]): Chip glances up for a moment, then looks down again and begins to read (Sound): "Very few suspect the existence of the city . . ." etc. (8 Sec's.)
11 (MS full figure [Continue from 7]): (Sound:) Chip continues reading. (4 Sec's.)
12 (FS): Pan across broken walls, burned beams, arches, charred ice box, twisted pipes in the recesses of the ruined buildings. (Sound: Chip continues reading.) (8 Sec's.)
13 (FS [Continue from 5]): In a wide shot of the ruined building, Chip sits in arch at the top of the brick mound, still reading. (10 Sec's.)

It took me less than ten minutes to write out the above 72 seconds (approximately) of film — the bare minimum as it strikes me, for capturing the experience we all had of walking into that back yard, conjoined with the reading of the passage. With more time, I could certainly find more creative approaches. But if one decides on such a sequence, those thirteen shots and seventy-two seconds can be filmed either well or badly.

The reason for shots 1 to 4, for example, is not simply to position "Chip"; it is to hint at the ambiance of the place around him—hints that will be solidified and intensified in far-shots 5 and 12. The reason for shots 7 to 10 is not simply to establish the fact that "Chip" is reading, but visually to set the emotional tone the passage itself will have. These secondary reasons are not—and can not be—evident from a script alone. But if the director has a sense of them and bears them in mind, the whole sequence will work more powerfully than it will if he loses sight of those reasons.

The above thirteen shot sequence is an executive, bottom line approach that recreates the space, range, variety, and resonance of the location for the ordinary viewer. The reading of the passage itself takes thirty seconds. Establishing location and ambiance—the hidden nature of this urban ruin—takes forty-two. (Film is, after all, a visual medium.) Once you conceive such a sequence, however, you have to spend ten to twenty minutes getting each of the thirteen shots. And without at least some notes in a notebook (each to be checked off as it goes "in the can"), you simply will not remember them all over the time it takes to film them.

And Derek/Terence had left his notebook back in the van.

Unfortunately, Moonlight got nothing even like the above on film. Nor, given what they did get, is there any way they can construct something near it. As effective as the reading was for the director and the crew, the range, space, and resonance of the location that set it off—the gate, the yard, the piles of brick, the over-all range of the ruined buildings—was never caught on film. All that was actually got were some close ups, some medium shots, and some far shots of "Chip" sitting in the window, reading—then standing at another location, reading part of the same passage. Thus, it's doubtful if it will register with anything like the power it had for the people there.

On the set of a well-made film, so much detail work has to get done, the actors are likely to have *no* idea of what's happening. That's because the transition shots take just as much time—or occasionally more time—than the "big" scenes:

The hand opening the window lock, the face straining through the glass, the foot braced against the floor, the window coming unstuck and flying up—each takes the same ten minutes to an hour to film as the five seconds of dialogue shouted out the window itself (dialogue that might well be filmed first). But it's often the three-to-four-second, four-shot sequence of the character straining so hard to open the window before delivering the line shouted through the open frame that creates the filmic performance. In such a situation, the actor will lose all sense of dramatic proportion and narrative logic.

It's the director's job to keep precisely that logic in mind.

But what was so dispiriting about the Moonlight shoot was how easily I could follow *exactly* what was going on—and even more, what wasn't. I had no sense of endless details being filmed that didn't relate (to me, the central performer), which, in general, is the feeling a competent film being put together by a director who knows what he's doing gives performers. On a small-crew (i.e., ten or under) sixteen-millimeter shoot like this, performers should feel that there is more being filmed around them than they could possibly understand—not a good deal less.

Still, there may be a ghost of that wonderful Harlem ruin, somewhere in what they got. But what saddens me is that we were *not* getting sequences, merely film—not because the director wanted something else, but because it was pretty clear the director didn't know *what* he wanted. And when, from time to time, he would get an inkling, in the very next minutes he would be so overwhelmed by details, he couldn't retain it.

Even at the professional level, this is sadly what most documentary filming turns out to be—just as, finally, most professional writing is only minimally competent, often for like reasons.

At any rate, Dave slugged up and down those bricks canyons with ten thousand dollars worth of camera on his shoulder and John beside him, with a hand-held spot "to wipe out some of the shadows."

Holding on to walls that, themselves, were none too solid, I came tip-toeing after, thinking: "Now I understand how John broke his foot!" What, I wondered, would their insurance people have made of all this clambering around, clearly in places man was not meant to go . . . But the general attitude seemed to be:

Anything for art.

Though, when, a couple times, I nearly sprained an ankle, I found myself wondering: Now just what has Art done for me, lately?

By the time we finished, it was almost dark.

What about the Brooklyn Bridge?

Not enough light. But the director had been thinking about some special effects sequences, down at Times Square—unless I was too tired . . . ?

Sure, I said. Let's do it . . . !

Derek/Terence seemed both surprised and grateful for my coopera-tion. But, back in 1973, I'd directed my own film (*The Orchid*), and I was simply trying to be like the wonderfully cooperative performers I'd been blessed with on my own shoot.

"What about our camera man," Karen wanted to know. "You'd had this all figured out with John. But he's not with us now . . ."

"Well, maybe Dave can do it."

What was it?

It was a time-lapse sequence the director wanted, at Times Square, with the traffic streaking around me in the darkness. We had three rolls of super-fast night-time film.

Said Dave: "Three months ago, I was shooting some time-lapse stuff down at Times Square . . ."

At which point we all laughed. But then, think of how many time lapse sequences at Times Square *you've* seen in how many pictures. It's *not* the most original idea in the world.

We drove down, in the bright-black New York night, to Times Square, and—it could only happen to a foreign TV crew completely unacquainted with the ways of New York—Keith found a parking spot, within five sec-onds, at 45th and Broadway. (I'd say your chances of finding such a thing are about the same as your chances of finding a three carat diamond on the sidewalk outside your house. I mean, it *happens*—but rarely.)

When we got there, at about eight, two other film crews had already set up and were at work; and half a dozen still photographers were also around, snapping shots—maybe half of them tourists.

While our folks lugged their cameras and tripods and lens-cases across Broadway, out to the concrete triangle that is the "square" it-self, I stood around waiting, watching one photographer, working on a picture for an album cover (he explained curtly, when I asked), with a black musician: the good-looking, middle-aged musician, in a kind of neo-zoot suit, leaned on the fence along the side, holding a white "phantom of the opera" mask in his hand with two drum sticks, up near his face. The picture (as I've described it) would have the all-too familiar iconography of Times Square at night a-glitter in the background.

We ended up back to back with a crew that was doing some night-time fashion shots.

The idea of the shot Terence/Derek wanted was that I would walk toward the camera at an extremely slow pace, while they took only a few frames a second or less. When shown at the ordinary speed of 25-frames-per-second, I would appear to be walking at normal speed — but the traffic and the lights moving around me would be hurling along at super-sonic velocities.

Sounded okay to me. But, once again, I was a little surprised at how unclear the director was on the actual mechanics of carrying this out. He wasn't at all sure how fast I had to walk. Or how long he wanted the shot to be. Or . . .

And he was also busy with Dave, the acting camera man.

So I got (lighting) John aside.

Look, said I. What he's got to know is: How long the shot should take in real time. Multiply that by 25, for the number of total frames he'll need. Then, divide total number of frames needed by the number of frames per second he's taking them at; and that will give you the number of seconds the walking should last in real time.

Makes sense to me, said John.

And Dave, who'd begun to figure out by now that John and I were the ones who actually had the information he'd need, rather than the director, turned his attention on me.

The director wanted to film at one frame per second.

But, as Dave explained to him, at that speed he'd get no moving background at all. The street would simply appear empty of traffic, with maybe a haze or a blur about. At three frames a second, he'd be speeding up the background motion by a factor slightly more than eight. A car passing at thirty miles an hour would look like it was zipping by at over 240 miles an hour. (At one frame a second, a car passing at 30 miles an hour would pass at over 720 miles an hour—that is, nearly eighty miles an hour over the speed of sound. You wouldn't see it.)

I added: If, in real time, one step takes me about a second, then—at one frame a second—I'll have to slow my walking down to one step every 25 seconds, which means the whole shot will take maybe ten minutes to film. But I don't know if I *can* fake walking that slow!

That seemed to satisfy Derek/Terence.

We timed the real walk—ten steps toward the camera, pause for four beats, then walk off, camera-left.

The ten steps took an easy 10 seconds; or two hundred fifty frames —which meant, at three frames a second, the ten steps had to be spread out over eighty-three seconds, i.e., approximately eight seconds per step.

We were doing this without sound; so, at my request, Karen counted seconds out loud for me, emphasizing four, eight, sixteen, twenty-four, thirty-two—taking half a step with each four.

We did it about five times.

Basically it was mime, was what it was.

At the end, the crew was congratulatory.

"It's nothing," I said. "A hundred pounds or so ago, I even used to dance . . ."

But I was rather impressed with myself, too. I'd neither fallen on my face nor gone down and skinned a knee. (*You* try walking down 42nd Street at eight seconds per step!) And, in one take, we got the obligatory group of three black teenagers, two girls and a boy, who tried to stop me and ask me what I was doing, then, after five/ten seconds (not quite one or two seconds of film), got bored and walked away, while I managed, though actually relating to them (I turned and looked very surprised, then turned back), to do it all in slow motion—so that if they want something humorous, it might well be usable.

And, in all of them, I think I got the swinging arms timed to my moving feet, so that, if it comes out at all, I probably look like a reasonable facsimile of a walking man.

We'll see.

That was it for the day. "If you want me tomorrow . . . ?" (It was about 9:35 at night.) "Now, I've got to be on the twelve o'clock bus back up to Amherst." (A white lie: the bus actually left at 1:30, but given their general time table till now—everything happening at least an hour late—that just seemed self preservation.) "But I get up early. You can have me from five in the morning till eleven. Then I'll have to scoot—"

Derek/Terence smiled. "But we don't have a camera man, for that time."

Apparently Dave was not going to be available to spell John tomorrow.

And the talk now was all of getting an extension from England, so they could take Monday and/or Tuesday to get the Comic Book artists they'd wanted.

"We can give you a lift home . . . ?"

"No thanks," I said. "I'm about three blocks away from one of my favorite bars. I'm going to drop in, have a drink. Then I go home and go to bed."

I shook hands with Paul, John, the director, Dave, kissed Karen and Sue, turned, and loped off across Broadway, toward Forty-Sixth Street.

On my way, I figured: they'd gone through nine ten-minute canisters of film that day—say a shy hour-and-a-half of actual film. The show they'd been commissioned to do was to run 28 minutes, though Terence/Derek was talking about a 50 minute version as well, to distribute to PBS in this country . . . But, sticking with the BBC version, that meant: three writers and five comic book artists covered in twenty-eight minutes. They'll have to give at least half the time to the visual artists—if not more. That's (maximum) fourteen minutes divided between three writers; or, a little under five minutes apiece.

If I was lucky . . .

I sighed and turned down Eighth Avenue. Who knows, I thought. It might sell the odd book or two over there.

Cats is an Eighth Avenue gay bar, between Forty-Fifth and Forty-Sixth. When I came in, the first guy who came up to me was my old friend bearded Bill Carswell, rather a bear of a guy, who explained to me that he was working there now as the bouncer.

In the ecology of the gay bars between 42nd and 50th on Eighth Avenue, Cats has an (or is an) interesting ecological niche. On 48th Street, there's a bar dedicated to serious hustling, called Trix. Walking into Trix often feels to me like walking into a new boat show, where, if you're not going to write out a $3,000.00 down-payment check within the first forty minutes, while you're tolerated, you're not really welcome.

Cats is where both the Johns and the hustlers from Trix, when they get tired of the high pressure game, come just to relax. The names and even the locations change. Ten years ago, it was the Haymarket and the Fiesta. (In a novel called *The Tale of Plagues and Carnivals*, about AIDS, I chronicled several scenes in the old Fiesta—which was gutted and turned into a locksmith shop about a year later. The old bartender there, Jimmy, now works in Trix.) Cats is not the place one comes in and announces "I've been starring in a BBC film production for the last ten hours." Even to Bill (who lived with me for three weeks, in '87, when he lost his apartment in the city). Any show of *anything* is, there, taken as a profession of wealth—which turns your little three by three square feet of space into Trix.

As it was, we joked around with two of the young working guys, one, a rather good-looking kid, named Kenny, from Menken, Georgia, who was all too eager to go (but who Bill warned me, when Ken would nip off to the John, was (a) a crack head, (b) a rip-off artist, (c) and not to be trusted within the length of a ten foot pole), and, later, another much more homely guy named Dave, but who (at like pauses) Bill assured me was (a) honest, (b) very good at what he did, and (c) an all around nice guy. I assured Bill I wasn't interested in either one, but thanks anyway. Then, at about ten-thirty, I went outside and treated myself to a cab ride home.

Chris and Iva were already in bed.

And I, in a word, fell out.

I'd actually had notions of getting up and making the eight o'clock in the morning bus. But I was a little more bushed than I thought. Around nine, I actually felt like getting out of bed. The first thing I realized was that I'd left my little plastic bag, with Iva's hairspray and hair brush, back in the Moonlight van. After a shower, I made a call to a very sleepy Paul at the Mayflower.

Yes, they'd found it in the van last night. He's already left it at the desk with a note to give it to me, whenever I showed up for it.

I thanked him, took a quick cab ride down and back (leaving sleeping daughter and her boyfriend), and was back before eleven-thirty. I spent a half hour vacuuming, washing dishes, generally getting the house straight. Put a couple of books in my bag (George Steiner's *Real Presences*, Dennis Cooper's *The Tenderness of the Wolves*) and at twelve-thirty told a drowsy Iva: "Look, I'm on my way in a few minutes. You know how to close up the house. You get yourself back to your mom's this evening, and I'll give you a call."

At quarter to, I took the overnight and my briefcase downstairs and up to Broadway. I had so little with me, I could have managed on the subway. But, what the hey, I've got arthritis and I was tired: caught a cab downtown.

In the bus station, there were droves of people waiting at gate 25. And I've also got a four-and-a-half-hour, very crowded bus ride ahead of me, I added — however after the fact — to my various reasons for splurging on the cab.

There were so many people that, at quarter past one, they announced they were running three buses in place of the one. Those of us who were going to Amherst ended up on our own bus, which turned out to be only about half full.

As we pulled out of Port Authority, it began to rain.

By the time we were on the highway, it was almost as dark as evening. On the opposite roadway the spray made a car-high mist, through which the traffic shot like boulders through smoke, while spider webs of molten glass wove and rewove our windows.

Between Springfield and Mt. Holyoke, there was some sort of accident that brought traffic to a halt for twenty minutes. The rain had let up for a brief few minutes. Ahead against the gray sky, you could see billows of real smoke rising and roiling beside the road from the wreck in the distance.

Some while after a fire truck came by on the shoulder, we began to creep ahead.

The rain held back long enough for me to get my bags from the bus stop to the house. A very happy Dennis wanted to hear all about it; and so we went out to Amherst Chinese, and I regaled him with the details. When we'd got back home, the rain was thundering down into the street again.

On the phone with Iva that night:

"Gee, dad, when you told me you were going, I didn't realize you were *going*. I thought you were just leaving for a while."

"Honey, you know I had to be back for classes on Monday. When did you think I was going to go? Did you close the windows in my room?"

"Huh? Oh, no. I forgot."

"Oh. Well, maybe the rain wasn't coming in that direction. Would you stop over there in the next day or two and close the place up properly for me, like I asked you to . . . ?"

"Sure," just a bit curtly.

And the next morning (Monday), I was up and at the word processor by eight, back at Çiron.

That Monday, before I went to my classes, the text of Çiron passed 155 pages in length. So, on Tuesday, I took a deep breath, called Malcolm in England (Tuesday morning, Sept 17th; we are now back, in case you missed the transition, to the previous story): "Malcolm," I said, "I think one of the tales has turned into a novel—and had probably best be left out of the collection."

"I can't tell you how that idea delights me," Malcolm said. "It arrived yesterday. I spent last night reading and reading it over. I'm two hours away from sending the manuscript off to the costing department, now. And if it was a hundred-fifty pages shorter, it would certainly be a lot cheaper to print. And everyone over here would be happier—though, we all want to do it *your* way, Chip . . ."

"Malcolm," I said, "my way, at this point, is to take the Çiron man- uscript that you have out from the rest—and toss it in the garbage! It's two weeks further along anyway, and I'd just have to send you an alter- nate text, in any case."

"Will do," said Malcolm. And after a bit of further chitchat, we hung up, me feeling much relieved. I didn't even think to mention the TV show to him. But I'll drop him a note.

The next four days, it rained torrentially—on and off—in Amherst. That was followed by four of the most unpleasant, muggiest, wettest, slimiest days in my memory. Then we had a pleasantly mild, dry week- end, during which some friends, Sam and Leonard, came up from New York. And, bless them, they drove us out to the mall where (at Radio Shack) Dennis and I bought a VCR and (at K-Mart), both of us, some new jeans.

And, after making minuscule changes on another ten pages, I wrapped

Çiron up, put a backing board under it, wound it with big red rubber bands, and sent it off to my agent in New York. That was Saturday, September 21st — and Sunday, the 22nd, I started a new journal notebook.

I confess, five days later I still look at it now and then. I've even made one more change since. (Also sent out four further copies to various and sundry readers, who may well suggest more emendations. Like Valéry said: "One doesn't finish a work of art . . .") But the manuscript is dated: Amherst, Sept. 1991. And that won't change.

Dennis and I both have (and have had for the last three, rainy days) head colds, that, finally, more or less account for the inordinate length of this letter:

Once I drag myself to classes, drone through my lecture, and manage to get back home, this is all I've had strength to do. Also it retards, just a bit, the post partum (or post novel) depression I must finally face, now that Çiron is off to New York, and will soon, I hope, start the process of becoming a real book, with covers and everything.

But to drift back to our initial topic, if I may, i.e., Theory. Really, in your letter, Erin, you go right to the heart of the matter yourself. As a number of people are realizing, it's a fundamentally theological question: is God / transcendence / the numinous / life / the spirit / guardian of play, freedom, and anti-entropy in a primarily determinist universe? (If that's the side you come out on, basically you have to end up on the side of deconstruction — or something very like it.) Or is God / transcendence / the numinous / life fundamentally the spirit / guardian of order in a chaotic, random, and meaningless universe. (That side must put you out, eventually, against deconstruction.) Maybe, like the difference between Auden's Arcadians and New Jerusalemites (in his wonderful *Horrae Canonicae*), it's fundamentally a matter of temperament, rather than of logic.

Still, if you want to read a good argument *against* deconstruction, that takes the questions involved seriously, try George Steiner's brief and elegant book, *Real Presences* (U. of Chicago Press: 1989) mentioned above. Though Steiner is firmly against deconstruction, he knows (a bit more of) what he's talking about (than Lehman).

I don't agree with him; but one can respect his argument, even if one wants to argue back.

Well, the great oak in the front yard, that last year exploded in scarlet for the fall, was rather ravaged by Hurricane Bob a month or so back — as were trees all around the sides of the lawn. I'd been pretty sure it was in fairly bad shape for the last six months. But, this autumn, its leaves are simply crinkling up, brown and shriveled, in unhealthy looking clumps here and there among the dark green still holding to some of its healthier limbs. It's rather sobering to see such a brave old creature dying — it's at least two-hundred-fifty-years-old, which means it was a young tree of sixteen or so at the birth of William Blake. I went so far as to have a local tree service cost out how much it would run me to take the dead wood out and prune it: Because (one) it's so big and (two) because electrical wires run through it (so that all the dead limbs must come down on ropes, rather than be allowed to drop [though it's dropped three large limbs on its own in the past year]), it would cost almost a thousand dollars to prune and service that one tree.

Really, though, it's almost worth it!

But I can't afford it.

Lost our downstairs neighbor — that is, Mrs. Taylor's daughter, Debbie, who is my age, finally decided to put her 93-year-old mother in a nursing home, after she fell in the middle of the night and broke her arm. Back then, my daughter Iva was up here — though I was away in Seattle, teaching at Clarion. (Actually, that was just before Cleveland, as a matter of fact!) Iva was nobly helpful, I'm happy to report. A pair of male graduate students have taken over the place, whom Dennis and I haven't really met yet. And our across-the-hall neighbor, Mark, has decided the $550 a month rent is too much, and has returned home — at thirty-three — to live with his mother.

The *Callaloo* off-print version of "Erik, Gwenn, and D. H. Lawrence's Esthetic of Unrectified Feeling" was, alas, rather butchered. The part they omitted had all the sex and four letter words. But the full version will be an appendix to *Driftglass/Starshards*. So, when it comes out in a year or so, I'll send you a copy and you can read the whole thing.

Classes are back in swing. Last week I lectured on Blake's "Auguries of Innocence," Sturgeon's "Microcosmic God," and Bear's "Blood Music" (the short story, not the novel expansion) to 90 eager students: Worlds in grains of sand, that sort of thing. Then there's the first department meeting of the term. Next week it's more Sturgeon, with *The Dreaming Jewels* and *The [Widget], the [Wadget], and Boff,* a truly great little American novella.

A few days ago in the late afternoon, while we were sitting in the kitchen over coffee, I looked out the window and saw a raccoon in the top of a tree out in the yard, a young one, cleaning herself meticulously, first with one foot behind an ear, then with another. I called Dennis over, and we gazed at her, quietly, till she climbed down, surely to forage and fight away the evening through the plastic jungle of neighborhood garbage cans.

Tomorrow there's some writers conference at the University, where I must take part in a one o'clock panel on "Genre Writing." How sad they'll all be when they learn that writing is writing, and all of it is just as hard as any other.

A couple of nights back, Dennis and I sat at the kitchen table and, on Dennis's portable TV, watched the PBS production of *The Marriage of Figaro*, getting hopelessly caught up in that lust-saturated, chaotic, Oedipal chora, which is the Almaviva gardens and castle, and where such extraordinary elegance unfolds in the midst of it, both above and below stairs.

That same day, I'd given my kids their first quiz (on Octavia's "Blood-child," and Lucius Shepard's "Salvador") — and they got just a bit twisted out of shape. But I think they'll come round.

You must tell me a bit about Andrew; and I will write you tales of my wonderful, wonderful Dennis (a Brooklyn Irishman,[12] he), whom I first met when he was homeless and living on the streets of New York, where, indeed, he'd been living for six years . . . ! We've been together up here now almost two full years, and he's still my favorite topic. Makes me feel rather childish — in a way I enjoy!

My love to you both,

Samuel R. Delany

13. Through his father; German through his mother.

APPENDIX : LETTERS TO IVA

July 1984–August 1988

• • •

My grandmother (Sara Boyd) did most of the baby care in our house in Harlem, and the lullaby she used to sing to me went,

> Go tell Aunt Rhody,
> Go tell Aunt Rhody,
> Go tell Aunt Rhody,
> The old gray goose is dead.

> The one she's been saving,
> The one she's been saving
> The one she'd been saving,
> To make a feather bed.

> She died in the mill pond,
> She died in the mill pond,
> She died in the mill pond,
> Standing on her head.

> The goslings are crying,
> The goslings are crying,
> The goslings are crying,
> Because their mammie's dead.

> Go tell Aunt Rhody . . .

One night I was woken up and lifted from bed, carried out of the darkness and through the short hall with the walk-in closet and out into the apartment hall and down the stairs—I was in my aunt Dorothy's arms. It was all very hurried, and everyone seemed rushed, and possibly upset. Aunt Dorothy carried me down the steps, with Uncle Myles behind us. She carried me outside and got into the backseat of his car and Uncle Myles into the front. I must have been crying, because Aunt Dorothy began to sing a lullaby. But it was "Rock-a-bye Baby"—not the one that Grandma sang. And Uncle Myles drove us out to their home in Brooklyn, the house in which he lived with my cousins Barbara and Betty and his ward, James Shaw, who slept in the little room that had been (I assume now) a maid's room at the head of the steps that went into the upstairs. I don't remember arriving, so possibly I was asleep again.

In both our house in Harlem and in my uncle Myles's house in Brooklyn there were several sets of sliding doors—pocket doors, I learned only last year, is the term for them. In our home there was one set of double sliding doors. In my uncle's house, there were double doors and single doors. They saved space, and I recall standing by the phone table, by the sliding door into the upstairs living room, with the stained glass in it, while Aunt Dorothy sat at the phone table and tried to get me to say hello to my mother. I just stood there, however, and listened to my mother speaking on the other end, while Sweetheart (our pet name for Aunt Dorothy) urged me to say hello.

I've written about my homecoming in my autobiography.

Soon I knew that I was supposed to have been "cyanotic" at birth—a blue baby—and I was supposed to have to have been brain damaged, but there was no trace of it in terms of my development. (I'd been a forceps delivery.) I assume things had gone more normally with my sister. Though I liked to tell stories in school and sing songs (once I started to attend Horace Mann–Lincoln, a year or so later in the old building that had housed PS 125), and I was very bright, I couldn't spell to save myself, or remember how the letters went, even for overnight, whether there were double or single letters, whether it was a d or a b, a q or a p—though it didn't stop me from reading everything I could get my hands on.

In a few days they took me back to Harlem to meet my baby sister who had just been born. (That's a trip I have no memory of at all.) Though I remember thinking she was difficult and a nuisance, we are still close many years later.

184 West 82 Street

New York, New York 10024

July 20th, 1984

Dear Iva,

Hello!

You must have thought we'd forgotten you, since nobody wrote. But we didn't. We were all just very busy!

I'm working hard on my new book, and I've had to do a lot of running around because of the covers on the two that will be published this winter.

Yesterday, Ashley came up, changed the gas-pipe on the stove (it had sprung a leak) and Frank and I spent the evening talking and cleaning the thing, inside and out.

To clean it, you get this spray can full of lye (which is like a very powerful acid) and spray it all over the parts with burned-on grease and stuff, which all turns into brown, runny gook that drips and dribbles over everything—and you get a sponge and wipe it off.

You have to wear rubber gloves, or you can burn your hands with the lye. And it takes two or three sponges, actually, because even with rinsing them and wringing them out, pretty soon they just about fall apart—at least if you start out with a stove as dirty as ours was!

It was really *Yucky*—but also kind of fun. And it was very interesting suddenly to see the real color of the inside of the stove: dark, dark gray with little white speckles.

But there must be things like that (both yucky and fun) at camp, too!

A few days back I had lunch with Judy Ratner, from downstairs. We went to Broadway Bay, the restaurant you used to like so much. Judy had lobster and I had a chef salad. But while we were eating and talking, I told her how much you had liked the movie *Gremlins*, and she asked me if I thought Maya would like it too.

I said, "I don't see why not."

Judy said: "Well, I've got money today. I think I'll take Maya, later on this afternoon, when she gets back from day camp."

Later or that evening, when I was at the dining room table, working on my galleys, the phone rang, and when I sat down in the red chair and picked up the receiver, I heard a little girl say: "Hello . . . Chip?"

"Maya?" I asked. "Is that you?"

"Yes," she said. "I waited to thank you for telling my mother to let me see *Gremlins*!"

"Oh, did you like it?" I asked.

"Yes!" she declared. Then she laughed. We talked about it a little more. I asked her what parts she liked the best, and what parts she thought were the scariest. She wasn't too sure, because basically she had liked it all.

Then we hung up.

But I thought you might enjoy hearing about it. We're all going to see you this weekend: me, Frank, and guess who else? A surprise. No . . . couldn't keep this kind of a secret. Grandma Margaret is going to come up with me and Frank this year!

Me and Grandma (probably) will be spending more time at the camp this year than we have in the past. This year I've asked Frank to let you and me stay on the camp grounds and take part in the programs there more than we have before. Frank will go off when he feels like it. But we'll have you out at least for overnight and breakfast.

Even though I've been *very* bad about writing, I love you lots and lots; and I've thought about you every day.

You say camp is not as good as last year. But that it's okay. Maybe you could talk with some of the campers and get together and make some suggestions to Gregg about what might make it better. I bet he'd really appreciate it that you and the other kids were concerned.

Or maybe it was just because you were feeling bad that day you wrote me, because I hadn't written you. I hope that was what it was — and believe me, from now on I'll be much better.

I promise.

(I hope you're not "almost crying" now!)

Glad you like riding and tennis. I'll bring you a flashlight and your knapsack, and some paper, pencils, and envelopes. I love you lots and lots, and I'm really looking forward to seeing you on visiting day.

Hugs and kisses,

184 West 82 Street
New York, NY 10024
August 3rd, 1984

Dear Iva,

Well, as you can see, we're trying to be a little bit better about writing, this month. Let me know in your next letter if you've gotten your package from Frank and a letter or two from both of us.

The weather has been hot and muggy here in the city, and I'm just glad you're away at camp, where you can (one) go swimming and (two) sleep at night — it's got to be cooler where you are, at least in the evening. There are a couple of movies I've recently seen that I'm looking forward to taking you to, when you get home. One was called *The Last Starfighter* and the other was called *The Neverending Story*. I think you'll enjoy them when we go to see them. You're all enrolled for riding camp, up at the Claremont stables, so you'll have a rather fun week, I think, when you get home. As far as my own work goes, there seems to be lots and lot to do, and no time to do it in — and the weather is just too hot even to want to do it. This, I'm afraid, is going to be a rather brief letter. I have to write a couple more to various people about business. So I'll bring this one to a close after telling you

I love you lots and lots,
Samuel R. Delany

184 West 82nd Street
New York, New York 10024
July 16, 1985

Dear Iva,

Here, you've written me two letters, and I'm just getting around to writing you for the first time. Please forgive your old dad for not having written you in two weeks. But your mom, Grandma Margaret, and Frank all tell me they have sent you letters—so you haven't been entirely without mail.

My excuse? Well, on July 4th, three days after I put you on the bus, I took the Train-to-the-Plane out to Kennedy Airport (where I'd picked you up on your return from France only a week before!) and took a plane across the country to Seattle, Washington.

It was a six-and-a-half-hour flight, and the movie was *Beverly Hills Cop* with Eddie Murphy. You and I saw it together around the corner at the old Loews' Quad (just when the Six Theater was opening up next door). During the flight I sat next to a young woman of about 27 who worked in advertising and who was returning to Seattle for her sister's wedding. When we were landing, she gave me some chewing gum to help clear my ears. And while I was chewing away, suddenly a filling came out from one of my back teeth, and I had a large hole in one back tooth that felt *very* funny whenever I put my tongue in it!

When I got to Seattle, it was one o'clock in the morning, my time—but only ten o'clock at night, theirs. And it was still a little light! Three very nice young women met me at the airport and drove me to Seattle Community College, where I was to be teaching. And as we drove in, through the car window here and there I could see fireworks splattering sparks above the lights of the freeway and the city against the deep blue.

In Seattle, I was supposed to teach another bunch of "big kids"—which is what you used to call my class in Milwaukee. Eighteen of them, from about 21 years old to 65 years old, had come there to take a workshop in how to write science fiction stories, which I was supposed to tell them how to do. Each morning we had a three-hour class, then we all broke for lunch and, usually, came back for *another* one-hour of class in the afternoon. Then the students all went back to the dormitory to do homework the rest of the day—which meant writing new stories and, at the same time, reading all the old stories everybody else had written.

Before the first class, however, when I was having breakfast, I found that even when I bit down on something as soft as scrambled eggs, I felt as if someone were driving a nail through that hole in my tooth and into my jaw! So once the first day's classes were over, someone who lived in the city took me around by bus till we found a dentist who put another filling in my tooth. And, let me tell you, finding a dentist who will take you without an appointment for an emergency job, the day after July 4th, in a strange city, is *not* easy!

But I did it.

For the rest of the time, things went very nicely.

Once I went to a bar-b-cue, given by the brother of another science fiction writer who was teaching there, Arthur Byron Cover. (Arthur used to be a student of mine perhaps fifteen-years-ago, which was the last time I'd seen him. And there he was, thirty-five instead of twenty, and teaching the big kids just like me!) I also saw Joanna Russ and took her out to dinner. And on Thursday night, I read one of my stories at the college. The reading was in a big room, with over a hundred gray, aluminum folding chairs in it. And there were still people who had to stand, because so many came to hear me. But they had put my name up for a whole week on an electric billboard that stood at the corner of the college, where they advertised events at the school. So a lot of people knew I was there and showed up. It was a long story—I wrote it a couple of years ago, about some of the stranger things that had happened to John Mueller in his interesting line of work. It takes almost an hour-and-a-half to read through. So I'd had to rehearse it a lot; I'd work on it just as if it were a play where I took all the parts at once. That was so people wouldn't get bored in the middle and go to sleep.

I guess I did it pretty well. Everybody told me how much they liked it, afterwards. And most people stayed around for another forty-five minutes, after the reading was over, to ask me questions about science fiction in general and other stories I had written. I had fun.

The "big kids" in the class were very nice. Most of them, sadly, couldn't write very well—it wasn't just that they couldn't spell or put sentences together. They just didn't know how to tell a story. But perhaps I was able to suggest to a few of them what to look for in the world and on the page to make their stories better.

At any rate, I enjoyed myself.

There was one very nice woman in the class, named Lee Wood, who *did* know how to write stories. She also knew how to drive a truck. She had a tan one there, which she called "Toby." She and Toby drove me all around Seattle, which was very nice, because of my bum foot—which still hurts, though it's getting a little better. One of the places we visited was called "Under-ground Seattle." The old part of the city used to be much lower. But because the streets kept flooding, and the mud-puddles got so deep that kids and horses kept slipping into them and drowning, and because their toilets kept backing up and overflowing, the people finally had to raise the whole city up—which they did by burying the streets and the first floors of all the houses, so that what had been the ground floors now became the basements. But then they dug out around them, so that they had all these strange, underground arcades, where people used to go to do their shopping.

These only lasted a few years; finally they were filled in. But a few years back, the city decided to dig them out again and make a museum of the underground part of the city. Today you can walk around in the re-dug out tunnels, and get some idea of how the old, underground part of the city used to look.

It was lots of fun to see; and if you had a good imagination, you could picture how it all used to look sixty or seventy years ago.

I flew back to New York late Sunday night; and here it is, early Wednesday morning. (It's about six o'clock, A.M., now, as I'm writing you.) Most of the time in between I have been cleaning the house, which was still quite a mess from all the time we spent sewing name labels on your clothes, from before you went to camp.

But things are looking a bit more orderly. I hope you're enjoying camp this year. I wish I were some place I could go swimming every day!

I'm sending you some t-shirts, as you asked. (But I am *not* sewing gum and candy into the hems! *Really*, young lady!) I'll also try and stick in some comic books and stuff. Grandma, Peggy, and Frank are all coming up on visiting day to see you; I'm still not sure if I can make it. But whether I do or not, from now on you will get lots of letters from me for the rest of the summer. I promise.

I love you a whole lot and miss you all deep down inside,

Hugs and kisses,

Samuel R. Delany

184 West 82 Street
New York, New York 10024
July 8th, 1986

Dear Iva,

Well, I just got your first letter yesterday—and here I'm just getting 'round to sending you your stamps! Doesn't seem like a very good start I'm making. But I promise to do better.

The Clearasil will be coming soon.

The city has been paralytically hot, and I'm sure I haven't been able to do *anything* since you left!

The 4th of July weekend was quite something here in the city, though I didn't see much of it. On the morning of the 4th, Ed Summer called me up to ask if I was going down to Riverside Park to look at the vast parade of boats from all over the world sail up the river.

So, about eleven, I stopped work and went over to Riverside Park to watch for about an hour. There were thousands of people there. But I ended up just two rows away from the railing by the water, toward the end of the walkway just above the marina where the boats park at 79th Street; the first boat to come up the river was the fireboat, which was spraying five jets of water into the air, kind of like a reverse Niagara Falls.

That was impressive.

But the others came so slowly, and were so far away across the Hudson, that after an hour I went back home and started to work. I saw three big boats in all that time! (And ten or twelve tiny ones.) The fireworks this year were down at Battery Park, so nothing was going on up here at Central Park in our neighborhood, the way it has other years. Later that evening, I went to a movie on Eighth Avenue, just to get out of the heat. When I was coming out, at about 9:30, way, way down at the end of the city I could see a few fireworks going off, a few balls of expanding sparks like toys above the buildings three miles down.

And that was it, for the Fourth.

From the TV and the newspapers, you would have thought it was the biggest thing imaginable. And, for a lot of people, I suppose it was. But, then, for a lot more, it wasn't.

Well, this morning it's cooled off for the first time. And so I'm getting this off to you.

Tomorrow at 10:00 I talk to a creative writing class at the New School down on 12th Street.

I found your comments on shaved legs quite interesting. It would seem to me that there wouldn't be anyone there, up at camp, you had to shave your legs *for*. Really, it just seems like more trouble than it's worth.

At any rate, have a good time and enjoy yourself.

I shall try to do the same.

— Love,

5184 West 82 Street
New York, NY 10024
July 29, 1986

Dear Iva,

As you can see, I'm not writing this on my word processor. This is getting done at Arbor House, where I've been working three days a week for David Hartwell.

Arbor means tree, or grove of trees. And house means house. It would be nice if Arbor House were really a tree-house, or a house in a grove. But basically it's just an office, down on East 45th Street.

Yesterday, I spoke to Frank and mother on the phone. They said they had a wonderful time seeing you, up at camp. It made me miss you that much more, so I took out all my letters that you had sent me — four! And read them again. Then, of course, I realized that I had only sent you one! So this is a second, to make up for that, just a little.

But I must ask you: Did you get the package I sent you? It was all full of toys and activity books and such like. Both Frank and Grandma said you hadn't mentioned it to them — which, of course, made me wonder if it ever got there.

Do let me know if you got it, next time you write.

The heat in the city has been unbearable. Sometimes it isn't even that hot, but the air is so muggy and damp that you end up sopping wet anyway, just walking from one end of the house to the other, or going out to the store.

Because of the heat, not very much has been happening here in the city. The only real work I've gotten done — other than what I do here at the office — is send four or five big boxes of papers up to the Library at Boston University that collects my old manuscripts and notebooks and stuff. But it was enough so that you can now see the whole floor in my office. Still, the house is not substantially cleaner on the whole than it was when you left. If we get some cool weather, I'll try and clean it up before you come back.

The Sunday Frank and Peggy and Grandma were up seeing you, I went to the Studio Museum in Harlem and heard a young professor[1]

1. Henry Louis Gates Jr.

from Cornell, where I'll be teaching in autumn. He was very smart and he talked about several black writers who all, from time to time, mentioned characters, sometimes men and sometimes women, standing on the shore and looking off at sailboats. It was very interesting, the various sorts of things that the various writers described, while their characters looked at the boats and their sails.

Since you left, I've become fascinated with garbage!

I think I may even write a book about it.

One of the most interesting things about garbage is that everything turns into it eventually—almost.

And the day before yesterday, Greg Frux and I had dinner at a very nice Indian restaurant, downtown in the East Village, with a young sewage disposal engineer and his girlfriend. Matt, the engineer, is going to give me a tour through some sewers and show me around a sewage plant.

By the bye, we have computers in our office. And, today, they're down. I work in a little corner (literally—a small wedge just off the rest of the office and I am at the back of it, at the point) off the accounting department. It's terribly crowded—with books and desks and piles of manuscripts; and the air conditioner is in the window to my left, so that when I am sitting at the big desk working, the air blows directly onto my right shoulder. The only way I escape it is to work back at the tiny little table that is smaller than the typewriter that sits on it, and put my knees up against the side of the smaller desk. You wouldn't believe how uncomfortable it is. Arbor House is supposed to move to a larger set of offices—but that's been promised for more than a year now. And I probably won't be working there when the move actually happens.

(Oh, as you can see, I'm finishing up this letter at home on my own word processor. It's much more comfortable here.)

One funny thing happened a few weeks ago.

I had some friends over for dinner. One was a young man named Tom Weber, who had spent some time helping me clean my office at home and generally doing secretarial work for me for three weeks. He's twenty-two, very nice, and reminds me somewhat of a gerbil. (He moves very fast and a lot.) Well, he has some friends, Patrick and

Dear Iva,

As you ca/see, I'm not writing this on my word processor. This is getting
done at Arbor House, where I've been working three days a week for David
Harwell.

Arbor means tree, or grove of trees. And house means house. It would be
nice if Arbor House were really a tree-house, or a house in a grove. But
basically it's just an office, down in on East 45th Street.

Yesterday, I spoke to Frank and mother on the phone. They said they had
a wonderful time seeing you, up at camp. It made me miss you that much
more, so I took out all my letters that you had sent me--four! And read
them again. Then, of course, I realized that I had only sent you one! So
this is a second, to make up for that, just a little.

But I must ask you: Did you get the package I sent you? It was all
full of toys and activity books and such like. Both Frank and Grandma
said you hadn't mentioned it to them--which, of course, makes me wonder if
it ever got there.

Do let me know if you got it, next time you write.

The heat in the city has been unbelievable. Sometimes it isn't even that
hot, but the air is so muggy and damp that you end up sopping wet anyway, just
walking from one end of the house to the other, or going out to the store.

Because of the heat, not very much has been happening here in the city.
The only real work I've gotten done--other than what I do here at the office
--is send four or five big boxes of papers up to the Library at Boston University that collects my old manuscripts and notebooks and stuff. But it was
enough so that you can now see the whole floor in my office. Still, the
house is not substantialjy cleaner on the whole than it was when you left.
If we get some cool weather, I'll try and clean it up before you come back.

The Sunday Frank and Peggy and Grandma were up seeing you, I went to
the Studeo Museeum in Harlem and heard a young professor from Cornell, where
I'll be teaching in the autumn. He was very smart and he talked about several
black writers who all, from time to time, mentioned characters, sometimes men
and sometimes women, standing on the shore and kicking looking off at
sailboats. It wasn very interesting, the various sorts of things that the
verious writers described, while their characters looked at the boats and
their socks sails.

Since you left, I've become fascinated with garbage!

I think I may even write a book about it.

.One of the most interesting things about garbage is that everything turns
into it eventually--almost.

And the day before yesterday, Greg Frux and I had dinner at a very nice
Indian restaurant, downtown in the East Village, with a young sewage disposal
engineer and his girlfriend. Matt, the engineer, is going to give me a tour
through the some sewers and show me around a sewage plant.

By the bye, we have computers in our office. And, today, they're down.
I work in a little corner (literally--a small wedge juts off the rest of the
office and I am at the back of it, at the point) off the acoounting department.
It's terribly crowded--with books and desks and piles of manuscripts; and the
airconditioner is in the window to my left, so that when I am sitting up at the
big desk working, the air blows directly onto my right shoulder. ANGLXWMMM
The only way I escape it, is to work back at the tiny little table that is
smaller than the typewirter that sits on it, and put my knees up against the

Letter from Samuel R. Delany to Iva, July 29, 1986.

5184 West 82 Street
New York, NY 10024
July 29, 1986

Dear Iva,

As you can see, I'm not writing this on my word processor. This is getting done at Arbor House, where I've been
working three days a week for David Hartwell.

Arbor means tree, or grove of trees. And house means
house. It would be nice if Arbor House wre really a tree-house,
or a house in a grove. But basically it's just an office, down
on East 45th Street.

Yesterday, I spoke to Frank and mother on the phone.
They said they had a wonderful time seeing you, up at camp. It
made me miss you that much more, so I took out all my letters
that you had sent me--four! And read them again. Then, of
course, I realized that I had only sent you one! So this is a
second, to make up for that, just a little.

But I must ask you: Did you get the package I sent you?
It was all full of toys and activity books and such like. Both
Frank and Grandma said you hadn't mentioned it to them--which,
of course, makes me wonder if it ever got there.

Do let me know if you got it, next time you write.

The heat in the city has been unbearable. Sometimes it
isn't even that hot, but the air is so muggy and damp that you
end up sopping wet anyway, just walking from one end of the house
to the other, or going out to the store.

- 1 -

Theresa Neilson-Heyden. (They have a hyphen in their last name,[2] just like yours.) I've known them on and off for ten years now, and they only moved to New York City a few years ago. I've been meaning to have them over to dinner since they first came here to the city. And since they're also friends of Tom's, I decided that was a good reason to have all three of them over.

And I did.

And they brought a friend named Garry.

It was a very nice dinner. I made roast beef—and I grilled some to-matoes, with garlic and basil and crumbled bacon on top. They like to drink a lot of coffee, so I made lots and lots. Just after we had finished eating fresh strawberries and ice cream for dessert and were all sitting around joking and laughing in the living room, the lights went out!

It was dark outside. At first I wasn't sure if we had a flashlight. Finally I found one at the back of the kitchen counter. Because it was Sunday night, the super had gone home.

I went downstairs, and though I managed to get the key into the basement (from the people in the corner barber shop), I couldn't find our fuse box, to see if a fuse had blown and to put in a new one. Since the new stores opened up on Amsterdam Ave., they've done all sorts of work in the basement, putting up new walls, making new rooms, and generally moving things around. I haven't been down there to change a fuse in three years.

So I just couldn't find it.

I came back upstairs and told Pat and Theresa and Tom and Garry that we would just have to finish talking in the dark. And since we'd al-ready done all the eating we wanted to, that's what we did.

It was really very pleasant, sitting there in the living room, the five of us, talking of this and that; and every once in a while someone would shine the flashlight on one or the other of us to see our expression.

Finally, they all went home. And, in the pitch black (with just a flash-

2. This is an error. Patrick Neilson Heyden, Theresa Neilson Heyden, and Tom Weber shortly formed Anzatz Press, which published a monograph by Samuel Delany, *Wagner/Artaud: A Play of 19th and 20th Century Critical Fictions* (New York, 1988).

light), I went to the bathroom, washed up, then went to bed. And, in the morning, when the super, Julio, came in, I went downstairs. Julio showed me where the fuse box was; and I got the fuse changed.

You would have thought that would have been the end of it.

But next Thursday, when the *Little Magazine* was having its meeting, in the middle of things, the lights went out *again*!

This time, I went right down and changed the fuse; because now I knew where it was. When I did, David saw some sparks and heard some snaps from the extension cord that goes around the big door between the living room and dining room, where I usually plug the vacuum cleaner in. There was a short circuit there, and that's what had been blowing out the fuses and making the lights go out. So we unplugged the cord; I don't use it anymore. I've got to take it out, soon, so that somebody doesn't plug it in by accident and blow the lights again.

Now that I'm home, it's a lot easier to write about what goes on at the Arbor House office — because no one will look at the typewriter and read my letter while I'm up from the desk, taking a manuscript off to mail, back in the mail room, or looking for a sub-rights form attached to one of the contracts stored in the contract files out in the hall. You know, this is the first time I've ever really worked in a business office in my life.

I must say, it's a lot easier than the work I do myself. But, then, you were here the first days I was working there. And I told you all that.

The room I work in has three other people in it (along with three computer terminals). The people are basically the publisher's sales accounting department. Their job is to make sure books are sent out to bookstores, that the bookstores have good credit ratings (so that the publisher knows she will get paid [The publisher is a very nice young woman of thirty-three, named Eden Collinsworth, who has her office down and across the hall from us, among the various editorial offices]), to check on which stores have paid for their books and which haven't, and to call up about money when bills are overdue.

Stewart has the desk on the other side of the room from me. He's about twenty-eight or twenty-nine, and is married, but has no children. He and his wife go to rock concerts a lot. He comes to work in jeans, black or blue, and likes to wear shirts with no sleeves. He's very friendly — he likes sports, and the two men who run the mail room, Nick (who is stocky and Greek and serious) and Howard (who is black and good-looking and tells a lot of silly jokes), always stop to sit on the edge of Stewart's desk and talk with him about this baseball team or that basketball game. Nice as he is, as he gets older, he's getting just a bit whiny —and he's very scared of all sorts of things. Once a big mosquito came into the office (which is on the 17th floor): Stewart squealed and ran into the bathroom, then lingered at the office door, peeking in, and refusing to come back inside until we got it out. Then he spent a long time telling us all how much he *hated* mice!

(Which is funny, because he likes horror movies almost as much as I do!)

The other man in the office is Walter.

Walter is one of the strangest-looking people I've ever seen. He's tall and thin—maybe six-foot-two or three, and his head is kind of wide and flat, rather like the top of a mushroom. He wears little round glasses with gold-wire frames that almost get lost on his broad, brown face. He's in his middle fifties, possibly even his earlier sixties. And he dyes his hair—he dyes it a dark brown, but it always looks very artificial and harsh and shiny. He apparently does it himself, and after a week or two, you can see the grey getting longer and longer through the thin patch at the back of his head, while he sits at the side desk, making phone calls or working at his calculator.

Now when you dye your hair, you're supposed to use rubber gloves, because your fingernails are made up of pretty much the same stuff your hair is. The dye soaks into the hair to color it. But if you don't have some covering on your hands, the dye soaks into your nails as well, and you'll end up dying your fingernails, too. While I've been working there, Walter has dyed his hair at least twice, and he must have forgotten to put his gloves on: both times he came in with his fingernails all dark brown—the second time in two bands across them, from where they grew out a little, before the new dye darkened them again.

For the first months of the summer, Walter always wore a suit and tie. With someone as meticulous as that, you'd think he'd brush his teeth. But Walter has very irregular, very long, bottom teeth. (I think the top ones are false.) He *doesn't* brush them, and all this white and greyish glop collects in the spaces between and around them, so that when he talks directly to you, smiling and telling you about a nice restaurant that's very inexpensive and you might want to try for lunch, it's . . . well, *very* hard to keep smiling back.

But I find myself wondering why he doesn't forget about his hair and pay some attention to his mouth!

I said that Stewart's voice was slightly whiney? Well, Walter's is *very* whiny! (Does Stewart ever wonder if he'll sound more and more like Walter as he gets older? Probably.) A lot of Walter's job is calling bookstores to ask them when they're going to send their money in: on the phone, he sounds just like a nagging mother. But before he calls, sometimes he sits for a moment and bites his lower lip, not wanting to make the call, not wanting to sound unpleasant. But he takes a breath, then punches the buttons for the number, and snaps out, "Hello, this Arbor House: and I'd like to know when we can expect your check for the money you owe us."

When he's not on the phone, Walter's very friendly and likes to talk a lot.

Much of my work is reading manuscripts to write reader's reports on them and fixing up badly copy-edited manuscripts. But Walter is a person who, without thinking about it, just assumes anyone who's reading can't *really* be working — even if they're reading a manuscript. So he's always trying to start a friendly conversation, when I'm at my desk, trying to keep track of the plot of some impossible SF novel.

A couple of times, without trying to be unpleasant, I've taken my work out of the office and down the hall to the big conference room (when there's no meeting going on), and working there, just so he won't interrupt me.

As far as I can tell, Walter lives by himself. He'll say to me, with his big, distressing smile: "I like to go home, make a few cocktails — have a couple of drinks, you know? And I put on the television . . . ? Last night, you know, I fell asleep in front of the TV and didn't wake up till *five* o'clock this morning! Isn't that awful?" Sometimes, when he talks about his life, it sounds terribly lonely; and I can't believe he has many friends.

But once, when we were talking, I mentioned you and told him how you were in camp in Vermont. Walter told me that he had a fourteen-year-old son, himself. But he doesn't see him anymore.

Since then, from time to time, he's mentioned things he and his wife used to do: they liked to drive through Vermont; and they had a little country house, once, somewhere in New England. And if you don't listen carefully, it sounds as if it was something they were doing together last week. But from many other things he's said, I know he was divorced quite a while ago. Now he lives by himself, somewhere just north of the city, and comes into work every day on the train.

The third person in our office is Renee. She's supposed to be both Stewart and Walter's assistant. She's perhaps twenty-three, and very pretty. I said Stewart and Walter are whiny. Well, Renee's voice is very soft and whispery and breathy—kind of like some of the characters Marilyn Monroe used to play. She's blond and wears pink blouses and, mostly, skirts—about every third day she comes in in slacks, usually white ones.

She's very dreamy and, while she's pleasant enough to everybody, she only really does what you tell her to. And if nobody tells her to do anything else, she'll just sit and stare at nothing with a kind of quiet smile on her face. Basically, I don't think she's really very smart. But it's hard to tell. (For about a week, all she had for lunch was a big bag of popcorn. That, I guess, was because she was on some kind of diet. But one, she doesn't really have to lose weight. And, two, she doesn't like popcorn. So she ended up giving it to Stewart and me.) As I said, the office where we all are is very small. Sometimes I have to put things on the floor, because there just isn't room on the desk. When Stewart gets the weekly printouts from the computer, he has to take hundreds of feet of carbon paper out from between the five interleaved copies, crinkling it up into a great big dark blue ball; so, he's often on his knees on the floor in the middle of the office, balling up long sheets of carbon paper and separating out the copies. But, somehow, Renee seems to end up working on the floor more than anyone else. I don't think, over a long period, anyone could really *like* that. Oh, for a single afternoon it might be all right, but after that I think you'd have to resent it. But she seems to spend more time on the floor than at her very small desk—I guess she has to, sorting papers, taking things in and out of folders.

For about a week, Stewart was very mad at Renee about *some*thing.

I'm only there three days a week, and whatever it was must have happened one day when I was out, so I never really knew what it was. But when I came in, Stewart was full of very harsh, biting jokes that had too much of an edge to them, mostly about Renee's stupidity. And every time she'd start to do something he'd asked her to do, he'd say, "Oh, never mind! *I'll* do it!" She must have done something that got him into some trouble. But his attitude made the office very unpleasant for a few days. Then, after a while—as I said, Stewart isn't basically an angry person, and he must have realized we all had to work there, so—he pulled it all together.

But through it all, Renee just sat on the floor, moving folders and papers around, looking kind of dreamy, as if none of it really bothered her. I don't know what she's really interested in; but, whatever it is, it's not her job.

Well, I've gone on for quite a while.

And, as of this week, though I'll be doing some work here at the house for Arbor House (reading manuscripts and looking over galleys), I don't really have to go back into the office, except to drop things off or pick them up. But it was really quite an education.

I've known these people—Walter, Stewart, and Renee, as well as several others who are more involved with the work I'm actually doing myself—for five weeks now; only a little longer than you've known your newest friends at camp. But probably I won't see any of them very much, ever again. Yet for the weeks I've been working with them I've been thinking about them and their problems and wondering what they were thinking of this, that, or the other almost constantly.

It's really rather funny.

One reason I'm actually getting around to writing you is because the weather is a little more bearable today. After three or four days of summer thunderstorms and/or showers, I finally put away all the clothes that were out on the living room couch—ever since you left for camp. And this morning's temperature is bearable.

The big movie this summer is *Aliens*. I've seen it four times already—because I went to see it by myself on the first day. Then people kept on calling me up, wanting me to go see it with them. Fortunately, it's good enough so that I didn't mind.

I love you a lot.

Again, let me know if you got the package.

Hugs and stuff
from your dad,

Samuel R. Delany

PS—I'm sticking in the envelope Dr. Beecher gave you to send her a letter. You left it here, and when I was putting away the clothes yesterday, it turned up.

—Love, again

Letter to Iva
at Summer Camp:
Thoreau in Vermont

184 West 82 Street
New York, NY 10024

July 14, 1987

Dear Iva,

Well, once again I'm just getting around to writing you—and you've already sent me THREE letters? The heat here in the city has been unbelievable! It's like walking around in wet, hot, oily cotton all day long. Really, it's hard to do anything—especially to write letters. Or anything else for that matter.

Your cat—Bumper/Kid, whatever—is doing very well. We really have quite a pleasant time together. Though I confess, every once in a while when he sinks his teeth into my big toe, I do think of him as your cat. But by and large he's been very good. The other day I looked at an old picture you'd taken of him, when we first got him. He's quite a bit bigger, now!

I haven't gotten you any of the things on your list. Indeed, I kept putting off writing until I could get some of them. But finally I decided that would not get a letter out any faster, so I am just writing anyway. But I haven't forgotten them.

One bit of not so good news. On the Third of July, Grandma Margaret was out to dinner with some old friends, and just as they finished eating and she was going to the ladies' room, Grandma got very sick. They had to take her to the hospital, and she's been there ever since. She had what's called a stroke—which means that part of her brain is not functioning right. Peggy and I go to see her every day. And she's comfortable—the hospital is air conditioned, for one thing. It's called St. Vincent's, and it's down in Greenwich Village, but she's supposed to go to another hospital today, called Mt. Sinai. We still don't know how long she'll have to be there. But we'll let you know how things are going with her.

One of the reasons I haven't written you is that I've been spending so much time with Grandma. It also means that my work has been going very slowly. But in a week or so, I'll probably finish the book for David Hartwell that was *supposed* to be finished two weeks ago!

Peggy and Frank are very anxious to see you on parents' weekend. They're really looking forward to it. You already know, I will be teaching in Seattle that weekend, but I'll certainly be thinking of you.

Do you remember when we brought the pizza over to Ed's and had dinner with him on his roof? Well, I went over there again, and this time he cooked some very nice (green) spaghetti and some wonderful lemon chicken; we ate out on his tar-paper covered roof, with skylights poking up here and there and all the plants sitting around and growing up their strings, while it got darker and darker over the tall apartments on West End Avenue and Riverside Drive, and finally the moon came out. His friend Connie was there, as well as another friend of hers, Sue, who knew lots about ancient Greece. She's writing a book on it. It was a very lovely evening.

I saw one very funny film, called *Innerspace*, and thought about you a lot. It's the kind I think you'd like. Now that I've actually written you, I will try to get some of the things you asked for. But it may take a little time. Perhaps Frank and Peggy can bring them up when they come.

It probably doesn't seem fair.

But that's the best we can do. I hope you're having a wonderful time up there. When the night gets cool, and you're going to sleep, think—for only a second, no more—of how hot and sweaty we all are down here in the city. And feel very lucky.

Lots and lots of love
from your dad,
Samuel R. Delany

184 West 82 Street
New York NY 10024
July 27, 1988

Dear Iva,

I can't tell you how much fun it was to see you on parents' weekend. David and Anne drove me back down into the city. Once we stopped at a small restaurant that seemed to be almost nowhere at all, with the sky kind of grey overhead when we went in from the car.

Then we drove on home.

It was quite dark when they dropped me off on the corner of Columbus Avenue and 82 Street. With the sleeping bag under my arm, I trudged up by the police station and the Ukrainian church, came upstairs, fed Bumper, and went to sleep.

I've had two movie days since I've been back. On the first, I went to see a charming French film called *Babette's Feast*. It was based on a longish story by a Danish woman who wrote it (in English) under a man's name, Isak Dinesen.

In a small, Norwegian village, two sisters who belong to a very strict religious sect live alone and try to do good works and help their friends. One stormy evening, a woman comes to their house in the rain. She's a French woman, and she's looking for work. She has a letter from a man who used to be an old friend of the sisters, asking them to hire her as a servant. Though they don't feel they can afford a servant, she tells them she will work for nothing. But if they don't take her on, she's afraid she will just die.

So they do.

Babette—that's the French woman's name—does all their cooking and cleaning. She saves them lots of money by being so economical. Babette's only connection back in France is that a friend of hers there has been buying her a lottery ticket every week and sending it to her.

One day after Babette has been working at the sisters' house for fifteen years, a letter comes to her from Paris. She's won ten thousand francs in the Paris Lottery!

The sisters are, of course, fifteen years older now, and they have grown quite dependent on Babette. But now that she has ten thousand francs, they are sure she will leave them, and they resign themselves to saying goodbye.

But Babette asks them for one last favor. The two sisters give a dinner every year for their friends. At these dinners in the past, Babette has cooked what they asked for. But now Babette inquires if she can cook them and their friends a real French dinner—moreover, she wants to pay for it with her own money. It's to be her present to them for letting her stay with them and work when she had nowhere else to go.

After being a little concerned, the old ladies finally say yes. But between themselves they're a still worried. They're not sure what a "real French dinner" will be. They've lived all their lives on the coast of Norway, and though they speak a little French, they have never been to Paris (the way *you* have); and they've only met two or three people in their lives who have.

They get even more worried when Babette goes away for four days to the capital of Norway (called, in those days, Christiana—though today we call it Oslo) to order special foods, wines, champagnes, and fruits. She returns with a cage full of live quail, a live sea turtle, truffles, goose-liver pate, cases of wine, a great lump of ice (for this is all taking place in the 19th century, before there were any ice boxes, when big pieces of ice had to be imported) and fresh pineapples. She's also bought dishes, glasses, silverware, and linen—for she's planned a truly sumptuous dinner and the old ladies simply don't have the utensils or the service to make it or even to eat it—unless Babette provides them.

Days before the dinner, Babette starts to cook.

She has to hire a young boy in the village named Erik to help her with the cooking as well as serving the wine and the food. By now, even the neighbors who will be coming to dinner are worried. What in the world will they be eating? Has the French maid gone a little crazy, that she is making all this strange and unbelievable food? They've only tasted very simple things all their lives—porridge and codfish and brown bread and beer. They've never seen or heard of some of the things Babette is making. But finally, because they love the two old sisters, they decide they'll come to dinner and no matter how strange and awful the food is, they will eat it and not mention how terrible it tastes—out of love for their hostesses.

The big day comes.

That night there are two unexpected guests—an old woman who lives in the neighborhood but who, in her youth, has had some experience of the world, and her nephew, who is visiting her. When he was a young officer in the army, he had spent a summer in the town and had even been in love with one of the sisters, but now he is an aging general who has been all over the world. He is curious what the little village that he has not seen since he was a young man will be like.

The soup is on the table, and they all go in to dinner—with its sparkling white table cloth and the beautiful dishes, glasses, and candlesticks. Indeed, in the movie, it looked to me like the table just before we all would sit down to Christmas dinner at Grandma Margaret's.

Very tentatively the people taste the soup.

The general and his aunt realize how good it all is, of course. And they say so. This slowly allows everybody else to entertain the suspicion that he or she is really eating some very good food. After a little wine, they all begin to feel very good. Old quarrels among them are forgotten. Those of each of them who have had little arguments with others of them for years now forget them and in the midst of all the wonderful food and wine, enjoy each other's company for the first time in years.

Young Erik, who is just sixteen, makes a few mistakes while serving the food (Babette has rehearsed him for hours so that he can do it properly), but only the General realizes it; and the dinner is so far above what he expected in the little town that it rather charms him.

The dinner goes on and on. And soon they are all having the most wonderful time of their lives—in just the way that real good food, if you surrender to it, will give you such pleasure.

Afterwards, in a warm glow, they all go out in their cloaks and coats, cross the tiny square—stopping to gaze up at the stars—then stroll home. The two sisters, after waving good bye, go into the kitchen to thank Babette. It seems, before she came (Babette now explains to them, as she sits, tired but happy, in the kitchen—and young Erik lies curled in the corner, snoring) that she used to be a famous cook in one of the most famous restaurants in Paris. And just once, she felt, she had to do something to let them know who she really was, what kind of culinary artist she had been, and what her art might do when it was presented to good people like them and their friends.

Will she be leaving them now? the sisters ask.

No, she explains. She can't.

But why?

She has no more money.

No Money . . . ?

Yes, she spent her whole ten thousand francs on that single dinner for a dozen of her employers' friends. Now, if they will let her, she will go back to being their ordinary maid, keeping their kitchen and making the food they are used to.

They are all very happy.

It's really a moving little film. It's slow, and beautiful. The camera lingers on all the images, so that you have time to notice all sorts of wonderful things about the harsh Norwegian town and the small, primitive kitchen in which Babette prepares her feast . . . just as if you were actually visiting — and no one was hurrying you to leave. I'm sure someday you'll get a chance to see it, and I hope you'll enjoy it as much as I did when you do.

It was a very grey and green movie, with now and again a blinding salmon sunset, or the marvelous colors — glistening browns, velvety burgundies — of *alebrot* (a peasant Norwegian dish) stewing in a black iron Dutch oven, or blood-dark wine falling into cut crystal in candle light.

The only problem was that, in the last fifteen minutes, one of my contact lenses decided to pop out. Fortunately it clung to my cheek, like a wet moth's wing. But I had to rush out to the theater's bathroom, with my hand over my face so that I didn't drop it, then try to put it back in.

I guess I put it in inside out, because when I went back into the theater, it didn't feel comfortable at all. So I went back into the bathroom, took it out again, and just put it in my mouth on the tip of my tongue), holding it there till the movie was over — and watching the last few minutes with only one eye.

I still liked it a lot.

Then I rode home on the bus — the contact lens still on my tongue tip, like a bit of Saran-Wrap that I kept on being afraid I might swallow, and one eye still about half blind. Once I got upstairs, in the kitchen I cleaned it, disinfected it — and put it back in my eye the next day.

A couple of days later, I saw three other movies: Eddie Murphy in *Coming to America*, Clint Eastwood in *The Dead Pool*, and (my favorite) Robby Rosa in *Salsa*. *Salsa* had lots of good dancing in it — but the story was sort of silly. Still, it was fun.

The weather has been paralytically hot — with, now and again, a rain storm in the late afternoon that doesn't really cool anything off.

It keeps making me remember my weekend in camp with you.

The night after the chicken salad and the deviled eggs, and the marshmallows with Gregg and Joan and Grisley on the field, as we slept in your empty bunkhouse, I remember, it rained hard around three o'clock in the morning. I woke up, to lie there in my sleeping bag, watching it get light through the window at the foot of my bed. I just lay and looked — at the three thin tree trunks and all the green leaves slowly growing more and more visible outside, and raindrops like down-flying gnats swarming across them. Or I gazed at the plank ceiling and the things old campers had written on the unpainted boards between the support beams or on the beams themselves — Iva, just lying there, with you asleep in your top bunk bed on the other side of the doorway, and me listening to the water hissing and bumping all over the roof, was one of the happiest hours in my life.

I think of you a lot.

See you in three weeks.

Lots of love from
Your Dad

184 West 82 Street
New York, NY 10024
August 1, 1988

Dear Iva,

One reason this letter won't be any longer than it is is that as I was sitting down to write, the phone rang and a young woman on the other end, calling from Philadelphia, reminded me I was supposed to be interviewed on National Public Radio this morning.

Vaguely I recalled making the appointment a few days before. "Wasn't I supposed to be at the studio at 11:25 . . . ?"

"No," she said. "You're supposed to be there at *ten* twenty-five."

"Oh, dear," I said. "I'm glad you called, then. But that means I'd better leave right now!"

It was quarter to ten.

So I loped past Bumper, who's taken to sitting most of the day in front of my bedroom door because the air conditioning leaks out from underneath it and cools his back; then I went out to Broadway, got on the subway (the station was as hot as any place I've ever been; stepping into the aluminum sided subway car was like diving into a cold pool), and went down to the National Public Radio studios on 2nd Avenue and 43rd Street.

I'd put on a blue dress-shirt, just out of the fresh laundry bag. But by the time I reached the air-conditioned studio, it was soaked through with perspiration. It couldn't have been wetter if someone had poured a water pail over me in the street.

Still, the interview went well.

A couple of nights ago, a writer friend of mine, Walter Abish, invited me to visit him and his wife for dinner. Cecile is an artist and photographer. Walter is a dapper, middle-aged man, born in China, who is blind in one eye and wears a black eye-patch, like a pirate. He's much nicer than any pirate, though. He wrote a book that's great fun and that I hope someday you'll read. It's a novel called *Alphabetical Africa*. All the words in the first chapter begin with A. ("Ages ago, Alix, Alvin, and Alva arrived at Antibes . . .") All the words in the second chapter begin with A or B. In the third chapter, all the words begin with A, B, or C. And so on, till in the twenty-sixth chapter, there are words that begin with every letter. Then, in the next chapter, he cuts out Z. In the chapter after that, he cuts out Y. And then X. Then W . . . Finally, in the last chapter (it's only a single two-page sentence) all the words begin with A again. It's quite amusing.

Cecile and Walter live in a loft on Third Street. There's no bell, so that when you visit them, you have to phone from the corner. Then they come down to unlock the door and let you up. I got as far as Great Jones Street—I knew, eventually, it turned into 3rd Street. But even though I'd lived in the neighborhood for nine years, I couldn't remember exactly where. So I called. They told me they were just on the other side of the Bowery. I walked on over, and there was Cecile, at the big metal door, letting some other people in who'd just arrived—including a young woman with a bicycle who also lived in the building. We all rode up on the elevator and got out in their loft apartment.

Besides Walter and Cecile, two other couples and me were at dinner. One man was a very small professor with a very large beard (quite as long and grey as you've ever seen mine), who, it turned out, had written a wonderful book about the novelist Joseph Conrad. The book was called *Joseph Conrad: The Three Lives*, and I'd read it a few years ago. Another young woman was a professor of English. She'd just won a Fulbright Scholarship to France, and she sat with her bare feet on the edge of the table pretty much all the time after dinner (her toenails were bright red) and told funny stories—though I think they might have been funnier if her feet had been on the floor.

Cecile took me into the back part of the loft that serves as her studio to show me some large, striking photographs of German cities she'd taken. She told me that, though there were no people in the pictures, the images bothered her. She was trying to come up with a way to display the images in such as way as to underline for the viewer the exact way in which they disturbed her.

Then we went out into the front, where the table was set for dinner.

We started with zucchini and yogurt soup: that's served cold and has lots of dill in it. Then Cecile brought out a *boeuf en gelée*, which is basically cold beef stew. Then there were vegetables and salad—and some dessert, and some wine; but I don't remember what kind for either.

The little professor with the beard apparently knew my name. I don't know if I ever told you about this, but a couple of years ago I was being considered for a job that involved even more money than I'll be making at U. Mass. The job was for a very prestigious endowed "chair" at the University of Buffalo. I had to go up and interview for it a couple of Aprils back. I didn't get the job—but I came in second, out of some thirty or forty people they were considering. Well, this man had also gone up to interview for the job—and hadn't gotten it either. So we talked about that.

But while we were talking, every once and a while I would hear someone mention the word "MacArthur" on the other side of the table.

The MacArthur grants are the most important awards you can get in this country, short of the Nobel Prize. They're awarded for writing, for science and math, or sometimes just to people who've been important in various social causes. Sometimes people call them "the genius awards." One man I knew up at Cornell, Skip Gates, had gotten one. And the last person I'd heard of who'd won one in literature—Joseph Brodsky—did get the Nobel Prize only a few months later! A great deal of money goes along with the MacArthurs—a good deal more than you get for the Nobel Prize—several hundred thousand dollars!

A couple of times that evening, I heard Cecile mention the "change in their economic status"—when suddenly it struck me: Walter must have recently won a MacArthur!

A couple of more dropped phrases convinced me of it. I was surprised that I hadn't heard about it before—but apparently I'd missed the news.

When everyone was leaving, I took Walter aside and told him: "This is awfully embarrassing, Walter. But I hadn't realized you'd won a MacArthur. Congratulations! Certainly there isn't any writer I know who deserves it more!"

He laughed. "Actually," he said, "I'm delighted you hadn't heard. It's probably why we had so much fun this evening, talking." Walter gave me a copy of a magazine in which he had an article (on a German novelist named Bernhard). Then he rode downstairs with me in the elevator. (It's not a self-service one; it's a clunky old green industrial elevator that requires someone who knows how to operate it—Cecile and Walter both do.) When I stepped out the door, I saw more than a dozen teenagers and young men and women across the street, pretty clearly involved with selling crack, smoking crack (a couple of glass stems were being passed around), and running after each other trying to make deals.

"Really, it's a little sad," Walter said. "But down here we live right in the midst of crack city."

I said good-bye, went off to the subway, and rode home.

The next day, I was talking to David Hartwell about it, and he told me that a few months ago, yes, he'd read that two writers had been awarded MacArthurs that year—Walter Abish and another one named Thomas Pynchon.

A couple of days ago I bought a red plastic imported German cat brush for Bumper. Pretty much every morning, now, I give him a brushing right after he eats his breakfast. We sit in the air-conditioned bedroom, I pull the small wire bristles through his coat, and he tries to bite the brush's throat and tear out its belly.

Sometimes he gets my hand. But it's just play. And, as you know, that's Bumper.

When I clean the hair off the brush, each morning I have a grey ball about the size of a walnut, which I throw in the toilet.

Mark Gawron is in town and tonight he's taking me out to dinner, so I want to get this off to you soon.

On Sunday (day after tomorrow) I go up to Wellfleet, Massachusetts, to visit Barbara Wise for a week and teach a writing workshop at the Castle Hill Truro Art Center. It should be fun. And I will keep writing you from there.

Lots of love,
From your dad.

184 West 82 Street
New York NY 10024
August 5, 1988

Dear Iva,

And how's camp holding up after all this time?

Are you swimming along through *Les Misérables*?

I bet whatever's going on, you're having more fun than I am, here in the city. Basically, to walk down the stairs feels like climbing down through bales of loose cotton soaked in hot oil—which keeps running down your face and arms and back and legs as sweat.

Last weekend, I took the train up to David Hartwell's in Pleasantville. The very last issue of the *Little Magazine* has finally come out. There won't be any more after this. But the whole staff, en masse, is moving over to a new magazine called the *New York Review of Science Fiction*. So we've all been working on that for the last week or so. While I was up, visiting, I got to go swimming in his neighbor's pool—and even sit for a while in his neighbor's hottub!

I did a thirty-page article for the new magazine on a play based on an SF novel by a man (who died a couple of years back) called Philip Dick. It was an interesting play. I just hope my article was half as interesting as the play.

I stayed overnight at David's.

On Sunday afternoon, we ate lunch on the porch with Pat and Alyson and Jeffery. Then David drove me all the way up to Boston, where he's teaching a science fiction writing class at Harvard this summer. He really wanted me to come up and lecture to his class, and this was the only weekend I could do it.

We stayed overnight at his parents' house in a little town call Duxbury. They're a very nice pair of elderly people, David's mother is perky and talkative, while his father is quite hard of hearing. I wonder if the reason his mother talks so much is because she's used to someone never really hearing her. But I liked her anyway.

The next morning we drove into Boston, over the broad grey waters of the Charles River, and into Cambridge.

I've only seen the Harvard campus once before. It's very much a city university—like Columbia or NYU. Only it's littler and prettier. And all the bricks in the buildings around the outside of the campus are red.

There's a nice museum there, run by Harvard, called the Fogg Museum—named after a Mr. Fogg. The front is all red (like everything else). Some years ago, Cecile Abish (Walter's wife, whom I wrote you about last letter) had a show of photographs there.

She simply called her show: "Fogg." Then, what she did, was come into the museum early in the morning and take pictures of the empty rooms with their display case and corridors, but with no people in, yet. Then she blew them up, very big, and hung them all around the museum, so that when people came in and filled the place up, what they were looking at was pictures of the place empty.

But that was a long time ago.

The first thing we had to do was go up to the school offices and get some xerox copies of the student stories that had been turned in the previous week—so everyone in the class could read and talk about them. Of course the Xerox machine kept on breaking down. David got quite frustrated. We almost didn't finish in time. But finally, with what we had waving out of David's briefcase, we ran downstairs, out across Harvard Yard, and into the building that housed David's classroom.

It was one of the newish buildings, from the sixties. It had lots of glass and lots of plastic-y walls and lots of aluminum window frames. The class was perhaps seventeen high school boys (and one girl) who had gotten special permission to take a college writing class this summer. They were very nice. But as I spoke to them (the night before I'd read a handful of the stories they'd written), I didn't get the sense that they were very smart.

Still, I enjoyed myself.

The class lasted two and a half hours.

After that, we went and had lunch at the Harvard Faculty Club, with another SF writer named A. J. Budrys, who is teaching another section of kids. We were joined by a young physicist in shorts and a brown t-shirt and also the head of the writing department, who has a beard and glasses and is named Victor something-or-other. He was very pleasant and kept on apologizing for the Xerox machine.

Afterward, David, A.J., and I went out to sit on the terrace of the faculty club. Some of the students from his class joined us (everybody in shorts, all very tanned, most with glasses) and we just talked with them informally for another hour or two.

There was one boy from Texas who only read Stephen Donaldson, John Norman, and Dray Prescot books. All of these are pretty bad books, and people had been telling him that, too. He'd never even heard of some of the good SF writers, such as Heinlein or Theodore Sturgeon. He was kind of embarrassed, and at one point told me that soon he'd learn not to like the books he enjoyed and would learn to like others.

I told him, no. That wasn't the point. There was nothing wrong at all with his liking the books he now enjoyed. Nobody wanted to take away his ability to enjoy what he now found fun to read. I explained to him that if he would work on his reading, and try some new books (and some new kinds of books), he'd learn to like more things as well as what he already liked.

But it's sad: too many people really are afraid that education will take something away from them — rather than give them something besides what they already have.

I hope I convinced him. I tried very hard.

Later we drove back to Pleasantville — with David leaving me off at the train in North White Plains.

I rode the air conditioned commuter back to the city.

Yesterday Barbara had a champagne and sushi reception at the new space she's rented to house the video-tape library she and Howard run, called Electronic Arts Intermix. It's on the 9th floor of a loft building on Lower Broadway. It was very nice — but very hot. (No air conditioning.) I met some of the young people who work there. They were quite an interesting bunch.

Julie was there — and wanted to hear everything about you. So I told her as much as I could about parents weekend.

John Del Gaizo says to say hello to you. So does Ed Summer. And Frank hopes you understand the reason he can't write is because of his hand — which is finally getting better. But everyone here is thinking of you.

Especially Bumper.
And, of course, I am too —

With lots of love,

Your Dad

THOREAU-IN-VT
RR #1 BOX 88
THETFORD CTR., VT 05075
(802) 333–9106
8/13/88

Greg Finger, Director
Joan Hollister, Director
Stefan Sage, Program Director

Dear Camp Parents,

By the time you receive this newsletter (with a greeting from your child on the other side, camp will be just about over). We want to fill you in on what's been happening here, and to call your attention to the enclosed flier with INFORMATION ABOUT YOUR CHILD'S RETURN TRIP HOME, as well as an IMPORTANT HEALTH NOTE.

The hot, humid, weather has continued, almost without a break. That's meant lots of time staying cool in the lake, with swim lessons just about completed. Between 8/3 and 8/18 we have 12 inter-camp sporting events scheduled (the basketball team just got back from Camp Billings as I'm writing), three canoe trips, three overnights (including a 5-day hike), and at least 6 day hikes! 30 campers went off to a summer stock production of Grease today, and there have been trips to crafts fairs, horse shows, and a science museum. The mornings have continued as beehives of activity in shop, arts & crafts, photography, video, drama, sailing, archery, tennis & other sports, horseback riding (with lots of trail rides), and lots more. Tonight is WOODSTOCK, our outdoor music festival, followed by an all-camp sleep-out. The campers are busy and happy—and here's what they've planned for afternoons & evenings of the week ahead:

8/14: Pick A counselor; Surprise Party
8/15: Beach Party; Drama Evening "Monologues & Movie Shorts"
8/16: Steeple Chase; Thief
8/17: Afternoon Like an AM (choice activities); Folk Dance
8/18: Afternoon Like an AM; Drama Evening— "Kids"
8/19: Final Clean-up and Packing; Dinner Banquet, Screening of camper videos, & Final Hoot.
8/20: CAMP ENDS. CAMPERS RETURN HOME TO YOU!

The other day, we took our two raccoon kits, Ben and Jerry, out deep into the woods and released them. They'd been running free at camp for a week, and it was clear that the time was right for them to go off into the wild. They had grown and matured—and so have your children. They've learned new skills, met new people, and experienced new cultures (e.g., during our international day held this past week).

It seems strange to be writing the end of summer newsletter now. Usually, by this time, the evenings are cool—and so are the mornings. But, we're still in the midst of July-like heat. However, the calendar does not lie, and we must accept the fact that our 1988 camp season has come to a close.

We've enjoyed this summer with your children. We thank you for letting them share it with us—and we hope you'll remain part of the Thoreau-in-Vermont family. We're planning our fall reunion for Sat. October 15th, at Arrow Park in Monroe, NY; we hope that you'll be able to join us.

Regards from all the staff,
Greg, Joan, Stefan

ACKNOWLEDGMENTS

The author thanks Alex Lozupone for help with scanning and converting the hardcopy text to electronic text; Bill Wood for help with proofing and text conversion; Nalo Hopkinson for writing the foreword; and Barbara Wise and John del Gaizo for pictures.

Samuel Delany is an acclaimed novelist and critic
who taught English and creative writing at Temple University.
After winning four Nebula Awards and two Hugo Awards, he was
inducted into the Science Fiction Hall of Fame in 2002. In 2013,
Delany was named the 31st Damon Knight Memorial Foundation
Grand Master by the Science Fiction and Fantasy Writers of
America. This is his second published collection of letters.
1984: Selected Letters (Voyant, 2000) was the first.

Nalo Hopkinson was born in Jamaica. She is the author of
six novels and numerous short stories. Her first novel, *Brown Girl
in the Ring*, won the Warner Aspect First Novel contest. She has also
received the Campbell and Locus Awards, the World Fantasy Award,
the Sunburst Award for Canadian Literature of the Fantastic, and
the Octavia E. Butler Memorial Award for impactful contributions
to the field of speculative fiction. She is a professor of creative
writing at the University of California at Riverside.